Illustrated Shakespeare

Macbeth

Editor: Neil King, Hymers College, Hull

Stanley Thornes (Publishers) Ltd

This edition is for Roger Shipton, valued colleague.

• Acknowledgements

The author wishes to acknowledge the help of his students, and particularly Brendan Hilberink, in the preparation of this edition.

The author and publishers are grateful to the following for permission to reproduce material:

Malcolm Andrew (all © Malcolm Andrew 1985), pages 3, 11, 12, 14, 16, 17 (middle), 23, 24, 32, 36, 38, 42, 43, 44 (top), 46, 53, 58, 63, 64, 71, 77, 80, 84, 90 • Sophie Baker, page 35 • British Library, pages 37, 60 (top), 61 • Laurence Burns, pages 28, 31, 44 (middle), 45, 59, 65, 69, 91 • Nobby Clark, pages 70, 75, 76 • Joe Cocks Studio, pages 7, 9, 30, 47, 87 • Columbia Pictures Inc./ British Film Institute, pages 13, 67, 93 • Donald Cooper, pages 15, 17 (left), 26, 68, 74, 78 • Fotomas, page 10 • Guildhall Library, page 52 • Jamie Hobson, pages 88-9 • Ivan Kyncl, pages 22, 27, 41, 44 (bottom), 56, 85 • David Liddle, pages 8, 18, 60 (bottom), 82 • Mansell Collection, page 6 • Alastair Muir, pages 40, 73, 81, 88, 92 • Gerry Murray, pages 19, 39, 48, 49, 62, 66, 79 • New Victoria Theatre, pages 21, 83 • RSC Theatre Collection with permission of the Governors of the Royal Shakespeare Theatre, page 86 • Nicholas Toyne, pages 20, 29, 50, 51 • Rick Walton, pages 17 (right), 57.

We would also like to acknowledge the assistance given us by the Shakespeare Birthplace Trust and the theatres whose productions of *Macbeth* we have illustrated.

Every effort has been made to contact copyright holders, and we apologise if any have been overlooked.

Notes and questions © Neil King 1989
Line illustrations © Stanley Thornes (Publishers) Ltd 1989

First published in 1989 by:
Stanley Thornes (Publishers) Ltd
Old Station Drive
Leckhampton
CHELTENHAM GL53 0DN
England

British Library Cataloguing in Publication Data

Shakespeare, William, 1564-1616
  Macbeth.
  I. Title   II. King, Neil   III. Series
  822.3'3

  ISBN 0-85950-765-3 (paperback)
  ISBN 0-7487-0100-1 (casebound)

Typeset by Tech-Set, Gateshead, Tyne & Wear
Printed and bound in Great Britain at The Bath Press, Avon

Contents

Preface to this Edition   4

Macbeth

    Act I   **6**

    Act II   **25**

    Act III   **39**

    Act IV   **57**

    Act V   **76**

Sixty Activities and Questions   94

Notes on Productions of *Macbeth*
  Illustrated in this Edition   96

RSC 1976

Preface to this Edition

One of the guiding principles of this edition of *Macbeth* is that the student must have some idea of the play in performance and be able to produce it in his or her own mind before close study of the text is possible. A literary experience of a play is only valid after a theatrical one.

Some observations:

> Ideally, perhaps, the practical and critical study of a play should go hand in hand.
>
> *Drama: Education Survey 2* (HMSO, 1967, page 24)

> I assume that 'activities' . . . will take place. Study of this [critical] kind cannot be profitably undertaken without an approach through drama which includes improvisation and enactment. It also needs a varied approach through discussion which includes, for example, a forum in which critical viewpoints are presented and compared by pupil-advocates, who will learn in the process how to use the critics critically. And the approach through writing should include full-scale projects (if possible co-operatively prepared) as well as production notes for scenes and other variations on second-hand critical essays.
>
> Peter Hollindale, 'Approaches to Shakespeare at A-level' in *Teaching Shakespeare*, ed. Richard Adams (Robert Royce, London, 1985, page 95)

> The teacher could try to introduce the theatre into his classroom and his classroom to the theatre. The more this is done, the more the student is connected to the play as a vital thing.
>
> Braham Murray [Theatre Director], 'On Your Imaginary Forces Work' in *Teaching Shakespeare*, ed. Richard Adams (Robert Royce, London, 1985, page 56)

> This theatre is too easily a world of convention and ritual, where actors observe the picturesque decorum of Great Drama. The test is to make the world of the play answerable to the ordinary, commonsensical questions which audiences apply to the world outside it. Bogdanov describes directing a recent production of *Romeo and Juliet* at Stratford. "During the scene at the Capulet ball, Romeo sees Juliet and asks a servant who she is, and the servant replies, 'I know not'. Now why doesn't he know?" asks Bogdanov. "He works there and the party is being thrown in her honour. So has he just arrived or is he outside catering or what? It's one line, a small part, but that question is the key to acting that small part properly and therefore making the world of the play believable."
>
> Andrew Rissek, *The Independent*, 2 January 1987

> Mention has already been made of the value placed on the individual response. Sometimes examiners are faced with thirty or so answers that cover exactly the same ground in an almost identical way. Credit is given to these answers on their merits – they represent diligence on the part of teacher and taught, but they are at best competent and often rather flat; in other words, they are not likely to qualify for the highest marks because their imaginative content is so small. This really reinforces the point that candidates should be encouraged to come to terms with the text and to develop their own responses to it. Candidates who are drilled through the text line by line cannot be said to have experienced the most lively teaching, and their attitude to Shakespeare might well be adversely coloured by the experience. There are lively and inventive methods, many of them the subject of other parts of this book; all the evidence shows that such lively teaching in fact enhances the pass rates – it certainly makes for more enjoyable study.
>
> Ken Warren, 'Examining Shakespeare' in *Teaching Shakespeare*, ed. Richard Adams (Robert Royce, London, 1985, pages 148-9)

> One of my colleagues, who engages in as much scenic effect as possible when reading a Shakespeare play in class, has been known to bring in a forest of potted plants from his home in order to create a moving Birnam Wood – a great deal of fuss, of course, but his pupils will always remember that scene.
>
> Neil King, 'Starting Shakespeare' in *Teaching Shakespeare*, ed. Richard Adams (Robert Royce, London, 1985, page 67)

> To sum up: nothing is ephemeral in a performance text. An individual sitting in an audience watching the performance of a play is continually working at making a synthesis of the many and varied signals being transmitted by the actors, the setting, the costumes, the gestures, lighting properties, sound effects and so on. You cannot single out any one of these signal generators and give it priority over the rest. An active reader must be aware of the interconnection of everything that is seen and heard in performance.
>
> Peter Reynolds, *Drama: Text into Performance* (Penguin Masterstudies series, Harmondsworth, 1986, page 100)

> The notion of relevance has partly invaded all areas of modern life: things are only interesting in so far as they can be mapped onto current problems, current issues. . . .
>
> If you've got to make Shakespeare 'relevant', then junk it. It should be self-evidently relevant with a very short introduction. You shouldn't have to bend it into Belfast or Beirut to show that it's important. I think there are ways of showing it's interesting and relevant, even though it's in the past; perhaps *because* it's in the past. You don't have to go the lengths of putting it in leathers or on motorbikes, and that doesn't mean doing it in wrinkled tights either!
>
> Jonathan Miller in an interview with Rex Gibson, printed in *Shakespeare and Schools*, Newsletter 3, Summer 1987

This edition of *Macbeth* has been specifically designed with GCSE Literature in mind, but many of the activities will also provide useful material for GCSE English response to written material and, of course, oral work.

The marginal notes to the text provide enough glossary to enable the average student to work out what is going on in the text. Words whose meanings have not changed significantly have not been glossed; they can be looked up in a dictionary. Where possible, commentary has been replaced by questions in order to lead students towards an understanding, rather than telling them what to think (see, for example, the notes to Act I Scene 7 lines 54-9 on page 23). The emphasis is on encouraging students to think and draw conclusions for themselves.

This edition is not a mere crib, and is most useful when studied with the teacher. There are plenty of marginal suggestions and questions along the way and at the end of the book, but there is a deliberate omission of the kind of critical essay which weighs down students and leads them to think that any critical response must be written in a particular style. However, as well as the newer activity-based work, this edition provides much (traditional) literary stimulus which is useful for those who will go on to be students of A-level English. I hope that I have not annotated the play to death (as is the case with some editions currently available), but that one or two of the best tunes have been left for the teacher.

Neil King

Macbeth

List of characters

Duncan, King of Scotland
Malcolm)
Donalbain } his sons
Macbeth)
Banquo } Generals of the King's army
Macduff
Lennox
Ross
Menteith } Noblemen of Scotland
Angus
Caithness)
Fleance, son to Banquo
Siward, Earl of Northumberland, General of the
    English Forces
Young Siward, his son
Seyton, an officer attending on Macbeth
Boy, son to Macduff
A Sergeant
A Porter
An Old Man
An English Doctor
A Scottish Doctor
Lady Macbeth
Lady Macduff
Gentlewoman attending on Lady Macbeth
The Weird Sisters
Hecate
The Ghost of Banquo
Apparitions
**Lords, Gentlemen, Officers, Soldiers, Murderers,
Attendants**, and **Messengers**

The Scene: Scotland and England

The opening of the play is mysterious and frightening. Who are these hags? What do they want with Macbeth, whom we know is to be the main character in the play? The Elizabethan audience were used to seeing such women persecuted, and sometimes condemned and executed. Witches meant evil.

SD **Thunder** created in the Elizabethan theatre by rolling cannonballs up and down on a floor above the stage area

3 **hurlyburly** noise and confusion of both the weather and the battle

4 **lost and won** the first of many contradictory statements made by the witches in this play Can you find another one in this scene?

5 **ere the set** before the setting

8 **Graymalkin** grey cat Witches often had a cat or other animal as their 'familiar', which supposedly assisted them in their evil acts.

10 **Paddock** a name for a toad, another creature commonly associated with witches

10 **Anon** at once, straightaway

11 Witches, being evil, would rejoice in making good things unhealthy and seeing the unpleasant as good. The play is full of contrasting images of light and darkness.

12 **filthy** This word is emphasised because it seems to be an extra word inserted in the rhythm of this line. Can you see how and why Shakespeare has created this effect? We cannot be sure, but it is possible that in the Elizabethan theatre fog and smoke were created by burning resin under the floorboards of the stage. Remember that there is a battle in progress.

SD **Alarum within** A trumpet call is sounded off-stage (that is, 'within' the Elizabethan stage buildings, behind the open platform stage). What effect does this noise create compared to those with which Act I Scene 1 begins?

1 **bloody** There are more than a hundred mentions of blood in the play.

2-3 as is apparent by his pitiful state, the latest news concerning the revolt (that is, he seems to have just come from the battle)

Note: **SD** = stage direction

What do you think is the dramatic importance of this opening scene?

Act I

Scene 1

A wild heathland. Thunder and lightning. Enter three **Witches**.

1st Witch   When shall we three meet again
In thunder, lightning, or in rain?

2nd Witch   When the hurlyburly's done,
When the battle's lost and won.

3rd Witch   That will be ere the set of sun.   5

1st Witch   Where the place?

2nd Witch   Upon the heath.

3rd Witch   There to meet with Macbeth.

1st Witch   I come, Graymalkin!

2nd Witch   Paddock calls.

3rd Witch   Anon!   10

All   Fair is foul, and foul is fair:
Hover through the fog and filthy air.

[They vanish]

Scene 2

A camp near Forres. Alarum within. Enter **King Duncan, Malcolm, Donalbain, Lennox**, *with attendants, meeting a bleeding* **Sergeant**.

Duncan   What bloody man is that? He can report,
As seemeth by his plight, of the revolt
The newest state.

In a group, read Act I Scene 1 in four different ways to try to capture these moods in turn: viciousness, gentleness, foreboding, grim humour.
Try other moods which seem possible. Then discuss which version you would like to use in a production.

Witches with familiars (seventeenth-century woodcut)

Malcolm   This is the sergeant,
Who like a good and hardy soldier fought
'Gainst my captivity . . . Hail, brave friend!   5
Say to the king the knowledge of the broil
As thou didst leave it.

Sergeant   Doubtful it stood;
As two spent swimmers that do cling together
And choke their art . . . The merciless Macdonwald –
Worthy to be a rebel, for to that   10
The multiplying villainies of nature
Do swarm upon him – from the Western Isles
Of kerns and gallowglasses is supplied;
And Fortune, on his damned quarrel smiling,
Showed like a rebel's whore: but all's too weak: 15
For brave Macbeth – well he deserves that name –
Disdaining Fortune, with his brandished steel,
Which smoked with bloody execution,
Like Valour's minion carved out his passage
Till he faced the slave;   20
Which ne'er shook hands, nor bade farewell to him,
Till he unseamed him from the nave to the chops,
And fixed his head upon our battlements.

Duncan   O, valiant cousin! worthy gentleman!

Sergeant   As whence the sun 'gins his reflection   25
Shipwracking storms and direful thunders break;
So from that spring whence comfort seemed to come
Discomfort swells. Mark, king of Scotland, mark!
No sooner justice had, with valour armed,
Compelled these skipping kerns to trust their heels,   30
But the Norweyan lord, surveying vantage,
With furbished arms and new supplies of men,
Began a fresh assault.

Duncan   Dismayed not this
Our captains, Macbeth and Banquo?

3 **sergeant** referred to elsewhere as captain
   Perhaps the words merely indicate in general terms
   that the soldier is an officer.
5 **'Gainst my captivity** against the attempts of the
   enemy to take me captive
6 Tell the king what you know about the state of the
   battle.
9 **choke their art** constrict each other's skill (in
   swimming)
10–12 **Worthy . . . swarm upon him** deserving the
   name of rebel, because of the many evil qualities
   (or people) that gather on him
   What does the word 'swarm' suggest?
13 **kerns and gallowglasses** lightly armed and
   heavily armed soldiers
   The Western Isles included all islands off the west
   coast of Scotland, including Ireland.
15 **Showed . . . whore** proved to be like a prostitute
   to the rebels (that is, showing favours for a short
   time only)
   all's all his efforts
17 **Disdaining Fortune** ignoring the favour's of
   Fortune (who was regarded as an unreliable
   goddess by the Romans)
19 **Valour's minion** the favourite of bravery (that is,
   Macbeth)
21 **Which** who
22 ripped him open from the navel to the jaw
   The imagery is particularly violent in this context, yet
   it comes from the harmless profession of tailoring.
   Look out for many other images of clothing in the
   play.
   What does this line tell us of the character of
   Macbeth?
24 **cousin** Macbeth is a kinsman of the King.
25 just as from the direction where the sun begins to
   shine (that is, the East)
26 **direful** terrifying
27 **spring** source
   In what way may lines 25–8 be seen as fatally
   prophetic for King Duncan? In what way does the
   mention of a storm remind us of the witches? How
   does the mention of 'shipwracking' point to the next
   scene?
28 **Mark** take good note
29 **justice** The brave ('with valour armed') Scottish
   forces have justice on their side.
30 **skipping** light-footed
   to trust their heels to run away
31 **Norweyan** Norwegian
   surveying advantage seeing an opportunity
32 **furbished** either 'repaired', or 'polished', or 'newly
   provided'

O valiant cousin! worthy gentleman

RSC 1976

35 as much as eagles are alarmed by sparrows, or a lion by a hare
What does this animal imagery tell us about Macbeth and Banquo?
36 sooth the truth
37 double cracks twice their usual charges of gunpowder
39 Except unless
reeking smoking, steaming (from hot blood – compare with line 18)
40 Golgotha the 'place of skulls' where Christ's crucifixion took place, and so a famous place of slaughter
41 Why do you suppose that the sergeant fails to complete the line?
42 cry the gashes are open, like a bloody mouth
43 your words and your wounds suit you
44 smack of taste of, and so 'indicate'
45 thane a Scottish noble rank
46 looks through appears in
46-7 So should . . . strange and so should a man look who seems about to speak of strange news
49 flout the sky wave in insulting defiance against the sky
50 make our men cold with fear
51 Norway the King of Norway
53 dismal an image of dark foreboding, like many in this play
54 Bellona's bridegroom Macbeth is here described as Mars, the Roman god of war, who was married to Bellona, the goddess of war.
lapped in proof clad in tested ('proved') armour
55 self-comparisons that is, a courage and skill which matched his own
In what way is Macbeth later to bear comparison with this man?
56 Point sword point
57 lavish outrageously insolent

> How would you dress Duncan if you were mounting a modern dress production of the play?

Sergeant   Yes;
As sparrows, eagles; or the hare, the lion: **35**
If I say sooth, I must report they were
As cannons overcharged with double cracks,
So they doubly redoubled strokes upon the foe:
Except they meant to bathe in reeking wounds,
Or memorize another Golgotha,   **40**
I cannot tell:
But I am faint, my gashes cry for help.

Duncan   So well thy words become thee, as thy wounds;
They smack of honour both. Go get him surgeons.

                                    [*Exit* **Sergeant,** *attended*]

Who comes here?

[*Enter* **Ross** *and* **Angus**]

Malcolm   The worthy thane of Ross.   **45**

Lennox   What a haste looks through his eyes! So should he look
That seems to speak things strange.

Ross   God save the king!

Duncan   Whence cam'st thou, worthy thane?

Ross   From Fife, great king,
Where the Norweyan banners flout the sky,
And fan our people cold.   **50**
Norway himself, with terrible numbers,
Assisted by that most disloyal traitor
The thane of Cawdor, began a dismal conflict,
Till that Bellona's bridegroom, lapped in proof,
Confronted him with self-comparisons,   **55**
Point against point, rebellious arm 'gainst arm,
Curbing his lavish spirit: and, to conclude,
The victory fell on us.

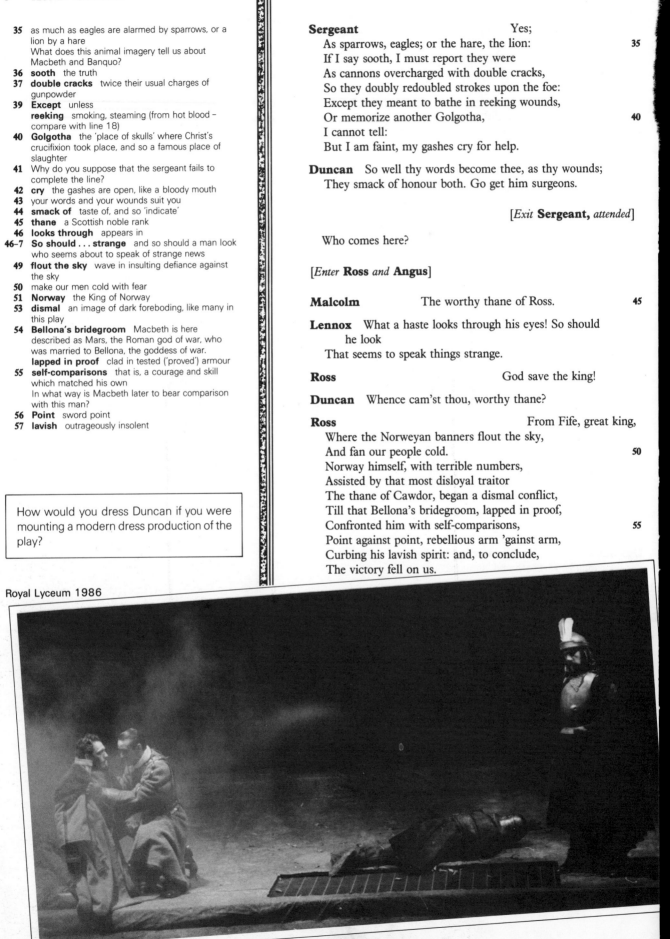

Duncan	Great happiness!

Ross   That now
Sweno, the Norways' king, craves composition;   60
Nor would we deign him burial of his men
Till he disbursed, at Saint Colme's Inch,
Ten thousand dollars to our general use.

Duncan   No more that thane of Cawdor shall deceive
Our bosom interest: go pronounce his present death,   65
And with his former title greet Macbeth.

Ross   I'll see it done.

Duncan   What he hath lost, noble Macbeth hath won.

[Exeunt]

Scene 3

A heath. Thunder. Enter the three **Witches**.

1st Witch   Where hast thou been, sister?

2nd Witch   Killing swine.

3rd Witch   Sister, where thou?

1st Witch   A sailor's wife had chestnuts in her lap,
And munched, and munched, and munched: 'Give me',
    quoth I.   5
'Aroint thee, witch!' the rump-fed ronyon cries.
Her husband's to Aleppo gone, master o'th' Tiger:
But in a sieve I'll thither sail,
And, like a rat without a tail,
I'll do, I'll do, and I'll do.   10

2nd Witch   I'll give thee a wind.

1st Witch   Th'art kind.

3rd Witch   And I another.

59 That so that
60 composition terms of peace
61 deign him burial of allow him to bury
62 disbursed paid
Inch island
63 dollars Dollars were not coined until Elizabethan times, 500 years after this story took place. Can you find another anachronism in this scene?
65 Our The king is using the royal plural.
bosom dearest, closest to my heart
present immediate
66 go to Macbeth and hail him as thane of Cawdor

2 Witches were said to kill farm animals out of spite in revenge for supposed insults.
5 quoth said
6 Aroint thee get out
rump-fed ronyon fat-bottomed (or well-fed in the best cuts of meat) scabby creature
7 Tiger a favourite name for a ship in Shakespeare's day
8 Records exist of criminal trials in which witches confessed to defying the laws of nature by sailing in sieves.
9 Witches were supposed to be able to turn themselves into animals, but could not give themselves tails.
10 What she will do to the sea-captain in revenge for his wife's rejection of her is unclear, but the repetition of 'do' suggests a determination to deal him lasting injury.
11 It was supposed that witches could sell winds.

RSC 1976

14 other that is, other winds

15-17 She controls the winds which can blow a ship away from ports to all points of the compass ('shipman's card').

18 Perhaps this means that the Tiger, driven by adverse winds away from all ports, will be unable to replenish her water supply.

20 pent-house lid eyelid (which slopes like a roof)
Who else will suffer from insomnia later in this play?

21 forbid cursed

22 sev'n-nights weeks
The witch will control the winds so that the Tiger is kept at sea for more than a year and a half!

23 peak, and pine waste away, and suffer

24 bark ship
Note that the power of the witches has its limits.

28 Bits of dead bodies were supposed to be valuable ingredients in making spells.

32 Weird an old word for 'destiny' or 'fate'
In what way may the witches be seen as connected with destiny?

33 Posters swift travellers

34 Presumably they are enacting a kind of ritual dance.

35 Thrice three times
Odd numbers, especially three, were considered useful in magic spells. Here the witches move three paces in the direction of each other in turn.

37 wound up complete, prepared
Does this suggest that Macbeth (and Banquo?) are already under an evil spell?

SD [Enter Macbeth and Banquo] The worlds of witches and of men, separated up to now, come together with the entry of the two generals. Indeed, Macbeth's first line is an unconscious echo of something we have heard before. Where?

39 called said to be
Shakespeare is probably trying to give Banquo a Scottish way of saying things.
How would you advise an actor to react after saying the word 'Forres'?

42 aught anything

43 question talk to
What does Banquo think they may be?

44 choppy chapped, shrivelled
Why, perhaps, do the witches react this way to Banquo, but speak immediately to Macbeth?

45 should be surely are

46 forbid . . . interpret prevent me from being sure

1st Witch   I myself have all the other,
And the very ports they blow,   15
All the quarters that they know
I'th' shipman's card.
I will drain him dry as hay:
Sleep shall neither night nor day
Hang upon his pent-house lid;   20
He shall live a man forbid:
Weary sev'n-nights nine times nine
Shall he dwindle, peak, and pine:
Though his bark cannot be lost,
Yet it shall be tempest-tost.   25
Look what I have.

2nd Witch   Show me, show me.

1st Witch   Here I have a pilot's thumb,
Wrecked as homeward he did come.

3rd Witch   A drum, a drum!   30
Macbeth doth come.

All   The Weird Sisters, hand in hand,
Posters of the sea and land,
Thus do go, about, about,
Thrice to thine, and thrice to mine,   35
And thrice again, to make up nine.
Peace! the charm's wound up.

*[Enter **Macbeth** and **Banquo**]*

Macbeth   So foul and fair a day I have not seen.

Banquo   How far is't called to Forres? What are these,
So withered, and so wild in their attire,   40
That look not like th'inhabitants o'th'earth,
And yet are on't? Live you? or are you aught
That man may question? You seem to understand me,
By each at once her choppy finger laying
Upon her skinny lips: you should be women,   45
And yet your beards forbid me to interpret
That you are so.

Macbeth and Banquo meet the witches (woodcut from Holinshed's *Chronicles*, 1577). What do you think of the image of the weird sisters shown here?

Macbeth   Speak, if you can: what are you?

1st Witch   All hail, Macbeth! hail to thee, thane of Glamis!

2nd Witch   All hail, Macbeth! hail to thee, thane of Cawdor!

3rd Witch   All hail, Macbeth! that shalt be king hereafter.   50

Banquo   Good sir, why do you start, and seem to fear
Things that do sound so fair? I'th' name of truth,
Are ye fantastical, or that indeed
Which outwardly ye show? My noble partner
You greet with present grace and great prediction   55
Of noble having and of royal hope,
That he seems rapt withall: to me you speak not.
If you can look into the seeds of time,
And say which grain will grow and which will not,
Speak then to me, who neither beg nor fear   60
Your favours nor your hate.

1st Witch   Hail!

2nd Witch   Hail!

3rd Witch   Hail!

1st Witch   Lesser than Macbeth, and greater.   65

2nd Witch   Not so happy, yet much happier.

3rd Witch   Thou shalt get kings, though thou be none:
So all hail, Macbeth and Banquo!

1st Witch   Banquo and Macbeth, all hail!

Macbeth   Stay, you imperfect speakers, tell me more: 70
By Sinel's death I know I am thane of Glamis;
But how of Cawdor? the thane of Cawdor lives
A prosperous gentleman; and to be king
Stands not within the prospect of belief,
No more than to be Cawdor. Say from whence   75
You owe this strange intelligence, or why
Upon this blasted heath you stop our way
With such prophetic greeting? Speak, I charge you.

[*They vanish*]

49 How do the witches know that Macbeth is thane of Cawdor?
50 **hereafter** in the future
51 Why *does* Macbeth start? Is this a sign of guilty thoughts? If so, what thoughts?
52 **I'th'** in the
53 **fantastical** imaginary, in the mind only
54 **show** appear to be
55 **present grace** his present title (that is, thane of Glamis)
56 that he will possess a greater estate of nobility (thane of Cawdor) and become king
57 **That ... withall** so that he seems entranced by what you speak
60-1 How do these lines help to show that Banquo is not reacting to the witches in the same way as Macbeth?
67 **get** beget, give birth to, be the ancestor of
How does the witches' response to Banquo differ from the one they gave Macbeth?
70 In what way does Macbeth find the witches 'imperfect speakers'?
71 **Sinel** Macbeth's father
72-3 Neither Macbeth nor Banquo appear to know of Cawdor's treachery. Was this discovered after they had left the battlefield? Or has Shakespeare been careless here? Would it matter to an audience?
74 **the prospect of belief** that which can be seen as credible
76 **owe** own, possess
intelligence news, information
78 **charge** order, command

Speak then to me ...

Leicester Haymarket 1985

79–80 Banquo says that the witches have vanished like bubbles.

81 corporal corporeal, of flesh and blood

84 on of
insane root Shakespeare appears to have had in mind a particular narcotic root, perhaps hemlock, henbane or deadly nightshade, which produced kinds of hallucination and madness. Shakespeare, being a countryman, was aware of the special properties of many plants.

86–7 Macbeth talks as if the witches' words are the theme from a song, and Banquo picks up the idea in the following line.
Might it be appropriate to support the witches' appearance with some kind of background music in production?

90 reads probably 'considers' rather than 'reads about'

91 venture daring

92–3 The king is so amazed by Macbeth's feats that he cannot easily find words to express his admiration; so he remains silent.

96–7 Macbeth is in no way aghast at the sight of the carnage he himself is creating. How is this ironic in view of what happens later?

98 post with post messenger after messenger

100 poured continuing the image of hail

102 herald . . . sight usher you into the king's presence

104 earnest pledge, promise

106 addition title
What effect is created by the fact that Ross's words closely echo those of the 2nd Witch?

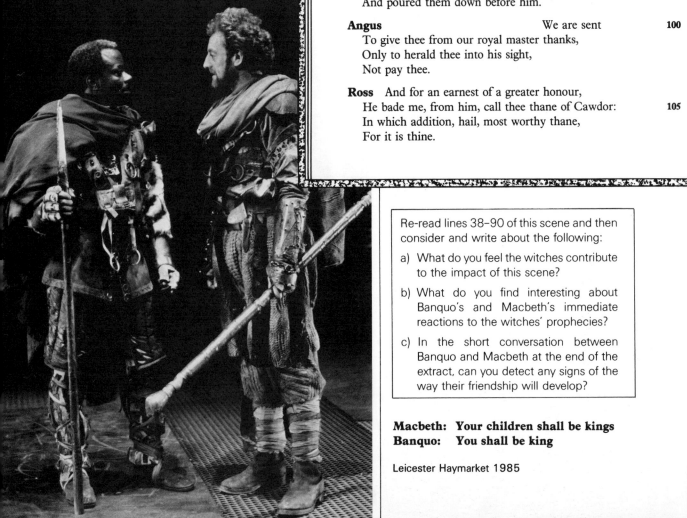

Banquo   The earth hath bubbles, as the water has,
And these are of them: whither are they vanished?   80

Macbeth   Into the air; and what seemed corporal, melted,
As breath into the wind. Would they had stayed!

Banquo   Were such things here as we do speak about?
Or have we eaten on the insane root
That takes the reason prisoner?   85

Macbeth   Your children shall be kings.

Banquo   You shall be king.

Macbeth   And thane of Cawdor too: went it not so?

Banquo   To th'selfsame tune and words. Who's here?

[*Enter* **Ross** *and* **Angus**]

Ross   The king hath happily received, Macbeth,
The news of thy success: and when he reads   90
Thy personal venture in the rebels' fight,
His wonders and his praises do contend
Which should be thine or his: silenced with that,
In viewing o'er the rest o'th' self-same day,
He finds thee in stout Norweyan ranks,   95
Nothing afeard of what thyself didst make,
Strange images of death. As thick as hail
Came post with post, and every one did bear
Thy praises in his kingdom's great defence,
And poured them down before him.

Angus   We are sent   100
To give thee from our royal master thanks,
Only to herald thee into his sight,
Not pay thee.

Ross   And for an earnest of a greater honour,
He bade me, from him, call thee thane of Cawdor: 105
In which addition, hail, most worthy thane,
For it is thine.

Re-read lines 38–90 of this scene and then consider and write about the following:

a) What do you feel the witches contribute to the impact of this scene?

b) What do you find interesting about Banquo's and Macbeth's immediate reactions to the witches' prophecies?

c) In the short conversation between Banquo and Macbeth at the end of the extract, can you detect any signs of the way their friendship will develop?

Macbeth: Your children shall be kings
Banquo: You shall be king

Leicester Haymarket 1985

Banquo   [*Aside*]   What, can the devil speak true?

Macbeth   The thane of Cawdor lives: why do you dress me
In borrowed robes?

Angus   Who was the thane lives yet,
But under heavy judgement bears that life   110
Which he deserves to lose. Whether he was combined
With those of Norway, or did line the rebel
With hidden help and vantage, or that with both
He laboured in his country's wrack, I know not;
But treasons capital, confessed, and proved,   115
Have overthrown him.

Macbeth   [*Aside*]   Glamis, and thane of Cawdor:
The greatest is behind. [*Aloud*] Thanks for your pains –
[*To* **Banquo**] Do you not hope your children shall be kings,
When those that gave the thane of Cawdor to me
Promised no less to them?

Banquo   [*To* **Macbeth**]   That, trusted home,   120
Might yet enkindle you unto the crown,
Besides the thane of Cawdor. But 'tis strange:
And oftentimes, to win us to our harm,
The instruments of darkness tell us truths,
Win us with honest trifles, to betray's   125
In deepest consequence.
[*To* **Ross** *and* **Angus**]   Cousins, a word, I pray you.

Macbeth   [*Aside*]   Two truths are told,
As happy prologues to the swelling act
Of the imperial theme. [*To* **Ross** *and* **Angus**] I thank
    you, gentlemen.
[*Aside*]   This supernatural soliciting   130
Cannot be ill; cannot be good. If ill,
Why hath it given me earnest of success,
Commencing in a truth? I am Thane of Cawdor.
If good, why do I yield to that suggestion
Whose horrid image doth unfix my hair,   135
And make my seated heart knock at my ribs,

107   What has Banquo decided about the witches?
108–9   Robes were a symbol of rank. Images of clothing
abound in the play. As the play develops, notice the
effect with which they are being used.
110   **bears** This verb suggests the weight of the
sentence of death which has been laid upon him.
111   **combined** allied
112   **line** reinforce
The rebel is Macdonwald.
113   **vantage** opportunity
114   **wrack** wreck, ruin
115   **treasons capital** acts of treason punishable by
death
117   **The greatest** that is, the most important title
(kingship)
behind follows after
pains trouble
120   **home** unreservedly, completely
121   **enkindle you unto** encourage you to burn with
desire for
123–6   often, in order to lead us into evil, the agents of the
devil (see line 107) win our confidence with small
truths in order to betray us in the great matters
which follow
127   **Cousins** friends, comrades (not necessarily
implying kinship)
Does it matter what Banquo is going to tell his
friends? How is the line important to the dramatic
progress of the scene?
128   **happy** fortunate
Shakespeare uses images from the theatre to show
how Macbeth sees himself as becoming king at the
climax of a great drama.
129   **imperial theme** that is, kingship of Scotland
130   **soliciting** urging, egging on
131   This is typical of the kind of equivocation which
goes on throughout the play, and which is begun
and encouraged by the witches.
132   **earnest** see line 104 of this scene
134–7   What is the temptation ('suggestion') that so
frightens Macbeth? Compare this with Ross's words
in lines 96–7 of this scene.
135   **image** This word (and 'imaginings' in line 138)
was an Elizabethan metaphor for theatricals and
acting.
unfix my hair make my hair stand on end
136   **seated** fixed

Polanski 1971

137   Against the use of nature   in an unnatural way
139   what is going on in my mind, where murder is, as yet, only imaginary
140   single   either 'weak' or 'entire'
140–2   function . . not   Dr Johnson, the great eighteenth-century writer and critic, rendered these lines as follows: 'All powers of action [function] are oppressed and crushed by one overwhelming image in the mind, and nothing is present to me but that which is really future. Of things now about me I have no perception, being intent wholly on that which has no existence.' Note that here is another one of the play's apparent contradications.
142   See line 57 of this scene
143   will have me   intends me to be
144   stir   taking action
Does Macbeth seem in control of his own destiny here?
145   strange   new
145–6   cleave . . . use   do not properly fit the shape of the body until worn for a while – another image taken from clothing
147   Macbeth means that what will be, will be, and the most difficult of days will run its course to the end.
148   stay . . . leisure   await your convenience
149   favour   pardon
wrought   troubled, agitated
150   forgotten   he is, of course, lying
150–2   your pains . . . read them   Using the image of a book, Macbeth says that their services to him are written down ('registered') in every page of his memory.
152   Let us   let us go
153–4   at more time . . . it   at greater leisure, when we have had time to think about it
155   Our free hearts   freely, honestly and openly

Against the use of nature? Present fears
Are less than horrible imaginings:
My thought, whose murder yet is but fantastical,
Shakes so my single state of man that function   140
Is smothered in surmise, and nothing is
But what is not.

Banquo   Look how our partner's rapt.

Macbeth   [*Aside*]   If chance will have me king, why,
     chance may crown me,
Without my stir.

Banquo   New honours come upon him,
Like our strange garments, cleave not to their mould   145
But with the aid of use.

Macbeth   [*Aside*]   Come what come may,
Time and the hour runs through the roughest day.

Banquo   Worthy Macbeth, we stay upon your leisure.

Macbeth   Give me your favour: my dull brain was wrought
With things forgotten. Kind gentlemen, your pains   150
Are registered where every day I turn
The leaf to read them . . . Let us toward the king.
Think upon what hath chanced: and at more time,
The interim having weighed it, let us speak
Our free hearts each to other.

Banquo   Very gladly.   155

Macbeth   Till then, enough. Come, friends.

                                                   [*Exeunt*]

Look how our partner's rapt.

Leicester Haymarket 1985

Scene 4

Forres. The Palace. Flourish. Enter **King Duncan,**
Malcolm, Donalbain, Lennox *and* **Attendants.**

Duncan   Is execution done on Cawdor? Are not
Those in commission yet returned?

Malcolm   My liege,
They are not yet come back. But I have spoke
With one that saw him die: who did report
That very frankly he confessed his treasons,   5
Implored your highness' pardon, and set forth
A deep repentance: nothing in his life
Became him like the leaving it; he died
As one that had been studied in his death,
To throw away the dearest thing he owed   10
As 'twere a careless trifle.

Duncan   There's no art
To find the mind's construction in the face:
He was a gentleman on whom I built
An absolute trust.

[*Enter* **Macbeth, Banquo, Ross,** *and* **Angus**]

                                                O worthiest cousin!
The sin of my ingratitude even now   15
Was heavy on me. Thou art so far before,
That swiftest wing of recompense is slow
To overtake thee. Would thou hadst less deserved,
That the proportion both of thanks and payment
Might have been mine! only I have left to say,   20
More is thy due than more than all can pay.

Macbeth   The service and the loyalty I owe,
In doing it, pays itself. Your highness' part
Is to receive our duties: and our duties
Are to your throne and state, children and servants;   25

SD   **Flourish**   fanfare of trumpets
  2   **in commission**   with orders to oversee the
       execution
       liege   lord
5–11   It has been suggested that these lines may be a
       reference to the execution of Sir Everard Digby, one
       of the conspirators in the Gunpowder Plot of 1605.
  6   **set forth**   professed
  8   **Became him**   was worthy of him
  9   **been studied in**   learnt by heart, rehearsed,
       practised – another theatrical term
 10   **the dearest thing**   that is, his life
       owed   owned
 11   **'twere**   if it were
       careless   valueless, of no worth
11–12   **There's . . . face**   There is no way of telling by the
       face what is going on in a person's mind.
       In what way is it dramatically ironic that Macbeth
       now enters?
 15   **even**   just
 16   **before**   ahead in credit and worthiness
 19   **proportion**   amount due
 20   **Might . . . mine!**   I might have been able to give
       to you
 21   **all**   everything I have and can give you
 23   **pays itself**   it (service) is its own reward
       part   as in an actor's rôle on the stage

> Rewrite in modern English lines 14 **(O**
> **worthiest cousin! . . .)** to 29 **(. . . full of**
> **growing.)**.

RSC 1982

23-7 Macbeth shows a clear awareness of the proper order and pattern of relationships which he is soon violently to overturn.

27 Safe toward either 'with a sure regard to' or 'to safeguard'

28-9 I have begun ... growing Duncan is using a gardening image in order to refer to the granting of Cawdor's title.
What does he mean here?

31 infold embrace

32-3 Banquo continues the gardening metaphor.

34 Wanton in fulness unrestrained and overflowing
hide disguise

35 drops tears (which are normally signs of sorrow, but are here of joy)
How would you advise an actor to interpret the dash in the text at this point? Note that the verse line is one syllable too short.

36 nearest It is not perfectly clear to whom he is referring. What do *you* think?

37 We Why does the king become very formal and use the royal plural here?
establish our estate settle the succession
At this time the throne of Scotland did not automatically pass to the eldest son, and the king could appoint as successor anyone near to him, who was then usually made Prince of Cumberland (equivalent to the modern Prince of Wales).

40 unaccompanied invest Duncan is saying that his son is not the only one to deserve new honours ('signs of nobleness'), and that all who deserve shall be similarly rewarded.

42 Inverness Would it be immediately clear to an audience that they are going to visit Macbeth's home?

43 which will put us yet further in your debt

44 Any activity (or, possibly, 'taking a rest') is hard work when it is not done in your service.
Is this rather straining politeness to the limit? Or do you think that this kind of courtesy would have been normal?

45 harbinger a messenger who goes ahead of a royal party in order to arrange accommodation
Why is Macbeth so keen to reach his castle before the king?

45-6 make joyful ... approach What ironic meaning may these lines have?

48-53 How does the language which Macbeth uses in this speech contrast with the way he has been speaking to the king?

51 black and deep Macbeth is self-aware: he faces up to the reality of his evil thoughts.

52 wink at close for a moment and not notice (what the hand is doing – that is, murder)
What equivalent phrase do we use today?
be be done (Again, he means murder.)

It has been said that darkness, even blackness, broods over the play. When you have gained a good knowledge of *Macbeth*, see how many more references, such as lines 50-1, you can find which create this effect.

Which do but what they should, by doing every thing
Safe toward your love and honour.

Duncan   Welcome hither:
I have begun to plant thee, and will labour
To make thee full of growing. Noble Banquo,
That hast no less deserved, nor must be known   30
No less to have done so: let me infold thee,
And hold thee to my heart.

Banquo   There if I grow,
The harvest is your own.

Duncan   My plenteous joys,
Wanton in fulness, seek to hide themselves
In drops of sorrow. – Sons, kinsmen, thanes,   35
And you whose places are the nearest, know,
We will establish our estate upon
Our eldest, Malcolm, whom we name hereafter
The Prince of Cumberland: which honour must
Not unaccompanied invest him only,   40
But signs of nobleness, like stars, shall shine
On all deservers. From hence to Inverness,
And bind us further to you.

Macbeth The rest is labour, which is not used for you:
I'll be myself the harbinger, and make joyful   45
The hearing of my wife with your approach;
So humbly take my leave.

Duncan   My worthy Cawdor!

Macbeth [*Aside*] The Prince of Cumberland! that is a step
On which I must fall down, or else o'er-leap,
For in my way it lies. Stars, hide your fires!   50
Let not light see my black and deep desires:
The eye wink at the hand: yet let that be
Which the eye fears, when it is done, to see.

[*Exit*]

whom we name hereafter
The Prince of Cumberland
Leicester Haymarket 1985

Duncan   True, worthy Banquo; he is full so valiant,
And in his commendations I am fed:
It is a banquet to me. Let's after him,   55
Whose care is gone before to bid us welcome:
It is a peerless kinsman.

[Flourish. Exeunt]

Scene 5

Inverness. A room in Macbeth's castle. Enter **Lady Macbeth**, *reading a letter.*

Lady Macbeth   'They met me in the day of success; and I
have learned by the perfect'st report, they have more in them
than mortal knowledge. When I burned in desire to question
them further, they made themselves air, into which they
vanished. Whiles I stood rapt in the wonder of it, came   5
missives from the king, who all-hailed me, 'Thane of
Cawdor', by which title, before, these Weird Sisters saluted
me, and referred me to the coming on of time, with 'Hail,
king that shalt be!' This have I thought good to deliver thee,
my dearest partner of greatness, that thou mightst not lose   10
the dues of rejoicing, by being ignorant of what greatness is
promised thee. Lay it to thy heart, and farewell.'

Glamis thou art, and Cawdor; and shalt be
What thou art promised: yet do I fear thy nature;   15
It is too full o'th' milk of human kindness
To catch the nearest way: thou wouldst be great;
Art not without ambition, but without
The illness should attend it: what thou wouldst highly,
That wouldst thou holily; wouldst not play false,   20
And yet wouldst wrongly win: thou'ldst have, great Glamis,
That which cries 'Thus thou must do', if thou have it,
And that which rather thou dost fear to do
Than wishest should be undone. Hie thee thither,
That I may pour my spirits in thine ear,   25

54–8 Duncan's speech is almost painful in its dramatic irony: he cannot know, as we the audience do, what has just been going on inside Macbeth's head (look again at lines 11–14 of this scene).
What gives the impression that Banquo and Duncan have been talking together while Macbeth has been talking to us?
54 **full** exceptionally
55–6 **in his . . . to me** I find the kind of satisfaction in praising him that I do in eating a fine meal.
56 **after** follow
57 **Whose . . . before** who has taken the trouble to go on ahead of us
58 **peerless** unequalled
kinsman Duncan and Macbeth were first cousins.

1 **They** the witches
Lady Macbeth has clearly already read part of the letter. How does this give a sense of life going on off-stage?
2 **perfect'st report** Either Macbeth means that his own experience is the surest proof, or he has made enquiries about the witches and their powers.
6 **missives** messengers
8 **coming on of time** future
9 **deliver thee** report to
10 **the dues of** your share in the
11–12 **Lay . . . heart** keep it secret
What might Lady Macbeth do with the letter which makes this image literally appropriate.
14 **shalt be** Lady Macbeth unconsciously echoes the 3rd Witch. Does she pause after 'be'? Was she about to say 'king'?
16ff Is Lady Macbeth's view of her husband the same as an audience's at this point in the play?
17 **catch . . . way** get what you want by the direst method
wouldst wish to be
18 **Art** You are
19 **illness . . . it** necessary wickedness
19–20 **what thou . . . holily** you want to achieve your ambition by playing fair
21 **wrongly win** gain what you are not entitled to
thou'ldst have you want to possess
22 **Thus** that is, murder
have it are going to possess the crown
23–4 **And that . . . undone** Lady Macbeth is saying that Macbeth is stronger in his fearfulness of doing the murder than in his desire to undo the murder when once done.
24 **Hie thee hither** hurry here
25 so that I may whisper things into your ear
Is this image evil?

Left to right: RSC 1982, Leicester Haymarket 1985, Torch Theatre 1986

26 and correct with my stern words
27 **round** crown (see Act IV Scene 1 line 88)
28 **metaphysical** supernatural
29 **withal** with
29 **tidings** news
30 Lady Macbeth's thoughts have been followed so swiftly by an opportunity for enacting them that she is completely taken by surprise.
How might the messenger react to the strength of her words?
31 **thy master** that is, Macbeth
't it
32 **informed for** sent word ahead so that we might make
34 **fellows** fellow-servants
had the speed of out distanced
35 **who** the other messenger (not Macbeth)
35–6 **more...make up** enough breath left to deliver
36 **Give him tending** look after him
37 The raven was supposed to be a bird of ill omen, often heralding death.
39 Is there any significance in Lady Macbeth's use of 'my'?
40 **mortal** deadly
She is appealing to evil spirits.
unsex me here take away from me all thoughts which are 'soft' or womanly
41 **crown** top of the head
top-full totally filled
42 **thick** so that pity cannot flow along her veins and reach her heart, where compassion ('remorse', line 43) lives
44 **compunctious...nature** natural feelings of pity, pangs of conscience
45 **Shake** disturb
fell wicked
45–6 **keep...and it!** intercede between the action (murder) and the intention to commit it
47 **for gall** in exchange for the bitterest vinegar
murdering ministers evil spirits who inspire murder
48 **sightless** invisible
49 **wait...mischief** assist in promoting the evil things in the world
50 **pall** shroud (a word which suggests death)
dunnest darkest
51 **my** It seems that Lady Macbeth intends to do the deed.
By this point in the play, who appears to be more evil – her or her husband? Think! – the answer may not be straightforward.
52 **blanket of the dark** Lady Macbeth's image may be suggested by the habit of decking the Elizabethan stage with black drapes when a tragedy was to be played.
Compare Lady Macbeth's words in lines 49–53 with Macbeth's in Act I Scene 4 lines 50–3.

And chastise with the valour of my tongue
All that impedes thee from the golden round,
Which fate and metaphysical aid doth seem
To have thee crowned withal.

[*Enter a* **Messenger**]

                                                What is your tidings?

Messenger   The king comes here to-night.

Lady Macbeth   Thou'rt mad to say it!   30
Is not thy master with him? who, were't so,
Would have informed for preparation.

Messenger   So please you, it is true: our thane is coming:
One of my fellows had the speed of him;
Who, almost dead for breath, had scarcely more   35
Than would make up his message.

Lady Macbeth   Give him tending;
He brings great news. [**Messenger** *goes*] The raven himself is hoarse
That croaks the fatal entrance of Duncan
Under my battlements. Come, you spirits
That tend on mortal thoughts, unsex me here,   40
And fill me from the crown to the toe top-full
Of direst cruelty! make thick my blood;
Stop up th'access and passage to remorse,
That no compunctious visitings of nature
Shake my fell purpose, nor keep peace between   45
The effect and it! Come to my women's breasts,
And take my milk for gall, you murdering ministers,
Wherever in your sightless substances
You wait on nature's mischief! Come, thick night,
And pall thee in the dunnest smoke of hell,   50
That my keen knife see not the wound it makes,
Nor heaven peep through the blanket of the dark,
To cry 'Hold, hold!'

> Rewrite in modern English lines 39 (**Come, you spirits...**) to 53 (**...'Hold, hold!'**).

Royal Lyceum 1986

[*Enter* **Macbeth**]

Great Glamis! worthy Cawdor!
Greater than both, by the all-hail hereafter!
Thy letters have transported me beyond   55
This ignorant present, and I feel now
The future in the instant.

Macbeth   My dearest love,
Duncan comes here to-night.

Lady Macbeth   And when goes hence?

Macbeth   To-morrow, as he purposes.

Lady Macbeth   O, never
Shall sun that morrow see!   60
Your face, my thane, is as a book where men
May read strange matters. To beguile the time,
Look like the time; bear welcome in your eye.
Your hand, your tongue: look like the innocent flower,
But be the serpent under't. He that's coming   65
Must be provided for: and you shall put
This night's great business into my dispatch,
Which shall to all our nights and days to come
Give solely sovereign sway and masterdom.

Macbeth   We will speak further.

Lady Macbeth   Only look up clear: 70
To alter favour ever is to fear:
Leave all the rest to me.

[*Exeunt*]

---

54 **hereafter**   of the future
She is thinking of how he will be greeted in the future as king ('all-hail').
What feeling may we get because she uses the same word as the witches?
55 **transported**   (i) delighted; (ii) carried my thoughts away
56 **ignorant**   unknowing (of the future)
57 **instant**   present
61 At this point Mrs Siddons, a great actress of the past, looked into her husband's (Macbeth's) face for the first time.
61–3 She says that it is too easy to see that something is on his mind (as we say 'he can be read like a book'). He must act normally and be welcoming and friendly in order to suit the present occasion ('time') and so deceive ('beguile') people.
66 **provided for**   In what sense(s) does Lady Macbeth mean this?
68 **into my dispatch**   under my management
69 **solely**   (i) absolute; (ii) for us alone
70 **look up clear**   appear calm and at ease
71 to change the look on one's face is always a sign of fear
70–1 In Elizabethan plays, the end of a scene was often indicated by the use of one or more rhyming couplets ('clear', 'fear').
72 What extra impact is given to this line by the fact that it is (a) added on, and (b) incomplete (there are only three of the five beats expected in a pentameter)?

Write the reply that Lady Macbeth might have sent her husband had he not arrived home so quickly.

Re-read pages 18 and 19. What aspects of the characters of Macbeth and Lady Macbeth are brought out here?

Crucible Theatre 1985

SD   Oboes   Go and listen to oboe music. What kind of mood does this sound give to the scene? In Shakespeare's day the musicians would have played in a gallery high above the stage.
torches   that is, torch bearers
1   seat   site
2   nimbly   freshly
4   temple-haunting martlet   the house martin, which likes to build its nest under the eaves of churches
approve   prove
5   By . . . mansionry   by building his much-loved home (nest) here
heaven's breath   wind
6   wooingly   delightfully
jutty   projection
7   coign of vantage   convenient corner
8   pendent . . . cradle   hanging nest for breeding in How are these birds contrasted with the Macbeths?
10   delicate   soft
11–14   The love . . . trouble   Duncan is saying that love can be troublesome in that one is in debt to the giver, but it is a blessed thing; and you should pray to God to show us how to be grateful.
16   single business   feeble service
16–17   contend/Against   compare with
18   house   household, family
those of old   those honours we have held for many years
19   late   recent
20   We . . . hermits   We will continually pray for you (like religious recluses).
21   coursed   chased (a hunting image)
22   purveyor   an official who went ahead of a king to organise his food (compare with Act I Scene 4 line 45)
23   holp   helped

Scene 6

Inverness. Outside Macbeth's castle. Oboes and Torches. Enter
King Duncan, Malcolm, Donalbain, Banquo, Lennox, Macduff, Ross, Angus *and* **Attendants.**

Duncan   This castle hath a pleasant seat; the air
Nimbly and sweetly recommends itself
Unto our gentle senses.

Banquo   This guest of summer,
The temple-haunting martlet, does approve,
By his loved mansionry, that the heaven's breath   5
Smells wooingly here: no jutty, frieze,
Buttress, nor coign of vantage, but this bird
Hath made his pendent bed and procreant cradle:
Where they most breed and haunt, I have observed
The air is delicate.

[*Enter* **Lady Macbeth**]

Duncan   See, see! our honoured hostess!   10
The love that follows us sometime is our trouble,
Which still we thank as love. Herein I teach you
How you shall bid God 'ild us for your pains,
And thank us for your trouble.

Lady Macbeth   All our service
In every point twice done and then done double,   15
Were poor and single business to contend
Against those honours deep and broad, wherewith
Your majesty loads our house: for those of old,
And the late dignities heaped up to them,
We rest your hermits.   20

Duncan   Where's the thane of Cawdor?
We coursed him at the heels, and had a purpose
To be his purveyor: but he rides well,
And his great love (sharp as his spur) hath holp him

Why does Lady Macbeth go out to greet the King? Where is Macbeth? Write, or improvise in pairs, a discussion between Macbeth and his wife which occurs just before she enters in this scene.

Lady Macbeth speaks with charming courtesy in this scene, but we know that she is horribly insincere. Write down what you think is going on inside her head from the moment she enters until the end of the scene. Show what she is thinking as Duncan speaks. You could copy out Shakespeare's words, interspersing them with her thoughts placed in brackets. You could then act this out, with Lady Macbeth's 'alter ego' talking directly to the audience.

Northcott Theatre 1986

To his home before us. Fair and noble hostess,
We are your guest to-night.

Lady Macbeth   Your servants ever   25
Have theirs, themselves, and what is theirs, in compt,
To make their audit at your highness' pleasure,
Still to return your own.

Duncan   Give me your hand:
Conduct me to mine host; we love him highly,
And shall continue our graces towards him.   30
By your leave, hostess.

[*Exeunt*]

Scene 7

Macbeth's castle. Enter a **sewer** *directing divers servants. Then
enter* **Macbeth**.

Macbeth   If it were done, when 'tis done, then 'twere well
It were done quickly: if th' assassination
Could trammel up the consequence, and catch,
With his surcease, success; that but this blow
Might be the be-all and the end-all here,   5
But here, upon this bank and shoal of time,
We'd jump the life to come. But in these cases
We still have judgement here: that we but teach
Bloody instructions, which being taught return
To plague th'inventor: this even-handed justice   10
Commends th'ingredience of our poisoned chalice
To our own lips. He's here in double trust:
First, as I am his kinsman and his subject,
Strong both against the deed: then, as his host,
Who should against his murderer shut the door,   15
Not bear the knife myself. Besides, this Duncan
Hath borne his faculties so meek, hath been
So clear in his great office, that his virtues
Will plead like angels, trumpet-tongued, against

25 Lady Macbeth is saying that everything belongs to
the King, and must be paid back to him at any time
he wishes. She uses words connected with
accounting, such as 'audit' and 'in compt' (on
account, borrowed).
30 **graces** favours
31 **By your leave** He is either asking again for her
hand, or to kiss her on the cheek, or to be led into
the castle.
If you were director of this play, how would you like
to see your actors end this scene?

SD   **sewer** chief servant
divers various
1 **If it were done** if it (the murder) were over and
done with (and no repercussions)
3 **trammel** bind up (as in a net)
consequence repercussions, reprisals
4 **surcease** death
that but if only
5 **the be-all ... end-all** the single action and
complete in itself
6 **But** only
Macbeth sees the time of a man's life as a
sandbank in a sea of eternity (and so washed away
eventually).
7 **jump ... come** risk judgment in the after-life
8 **still** always
that so that
10 **th'inventor** that is, the person who first
committed violence
even-handed impartial
11 **Commends** offers, recommends
ingredience contents
chalice drinking vessel
14 **Strong both** both strong arguments
16–18 The historical Duncan was in fact young, and an
ineffective king. For what dramatic reasons do you
think Shakespeare has changed his age and
character?
17 **borne ... meek** used his authority as king in such
a modest fashion
18 **clear** free from corruption

You may never (I hope!) have considered
committing murder; but you may have
agonised over whether to do something
which you know is wrong. Talk about it.
Write about it.

Why does Shakespeare have Macbeth
speak lines 1–28 alone, outside the
banqueting hall? The soliloquy shows that
he is only too aware of his motivation, and of
the reasons why what he proposes is evil.
How does this make the murder, when
committed, even more frightening?

New Victoria Theatre 1966

20 **taking-off** murder
21 Why is Pity personified as a 'naked new-born babe'?
22 **Striding the blast** riding on the storm (of protest at Duncan's murder)
     Cherubin angels
23 **sightless couriers** invisible winds
25 **That . . . wind** so that tears of pity (at the horror of the murder) will fall from so many eyes that the wind itself will be drowned
25-7 **I have no spur . . . ambition** It is only eager ambition which urges me on (as a rider might spur on a horse).
27-8 **Vaulting ambition . . . th'other** Macbeth is comparing himself with either (i) an over-ambitious horseman who rides too furiously at an obstacle and so falls the other side; or (ii) an eager rider who vaults too flamboyantly into the saddle, 'overleaps', and falls on the far side of the horse. Which reading do you prefer?
32 **of late** recently
     bought gained (by his deeds)
33 **Golden opinions** a shining reputation
34 **would . . . gloss** should be enjoyed now whilst they are shining and new
35-8 Lady Macbeth is comparing her husband with a person who promises to do something when drunk, falls asleep, wakes with a bad hang-over ('green and pale') and cannot face doing what he said that he would do.
39 **Such** as unreliable as your resolution
39-41 **Art . . . desire** Are you afraid to act resolutely in order to gain what you dearly want?
42 which you value as the most important achievement in life (that is, the crown)
44 **wait upon** accompany
45 **adage** proverb, which ran: 'The cate would eate fyshe, and would not wet her feete.'
     Can you think of another proverb which suggests that you must be bold in order to get what you want?
     Prithee, peace I pray you, be quiet.
     How strongly do you think Macbeth says this? Why?
46 **become** be fitting for
47 **is none** that is, he is superhuman – or a devil

Find an example on this page of Macbeth using an image of clothing and Lady Macbeth sarcastically following up the image.

There are many questions on this page of text. What dramatic effect do they build up?

The deep damnation of his taking-off;   20
And Pity, like a naked new-born babe,
Striding the blast, or Heaven's Cherubin, horsed
Upon the sightless couriers of the air,
Shall blow the horrid deed in every eye,
That tears shall drown the wind. I have no spur   25
To prick the sides of my intent, but only
Vaulting ambition, which o'er leaps itself,
And falls on th'other –

[*Enter* **Lady Macbeth**]

                              How now! what news?

Lady Macbeth He has almost supped: why have you left the chamber?

Macbeth Hath he asked for me?

Lady Macbeth   Know you not he has?   30

Macbeth We will proceed no further in this business:
He hath honoured me of late, and I have bought
Golden opinions from all sorts of people,
Which would be worn now in their newest gloss,
Not cast aside so soon.

Lady Macbeth   Was the hope drunk   35
Wherein you dressed yourself? hath it slept since?
And wakes it now, to look so green and pale
At what it did so freely? From this time
Such I account thy love. Art thou afeard
To be the same in thine own act and valour   40
As thou art in desire? Wouldst thou have that
Which thou esteem'st the ornament of life,
And live a coward in thine own esteem,
Letting 'I dare not' wait upon 'I would',
Like the poor cat i'th'adage?

Macbeth   Prithee, peace: 45
I dare do all that may become a man;
Who dares do more is none.

RSC 1986

Lady Macbeth   What beast was't then
That made you break this enterprise to me?
When you durst do it, then you were a man;
And, to be more than what you were, you would   50
Be so much more the man. Nor time nor place
Did then adhere, and yet you would make both.
They have made themselves, and that their fitness now
Does unmake you. I have given suck, and know
How tender 'tis to love the babe that milks me –   55
I would, while it was smiling in my face,
Have plucked my nipple from his boneless gums,
And dashed the brains out, had I so sworn as you
Have done to this.

Macbeth   If we should fail?

Lady Macbeth   We fail?
But screw your courage to the sticking place,   60
And we'll not fail. When Duncan is asleep –
Whereto the rather shall his day's hard journey
Soundly invite him – his two chamberlains
Will I with wine and wassail so convince,
That memory, the warder of the brain,   65
Shall be a fume, and the receipt of reason
A limbec only: when in swinish sleep
Their drenched natures lie as in a death,
What cannot you and I perform upon
Th'unguarded Duncan? what not put upon   70
His spongy officers, who shall bear the guilt
Of our great quell?

Macbeth   Bring forth men-children only!
For thy undaunted mettle should compose
Nothing but males. Will it not be received,
When we have marked with blood those sleepy two   75
Of his own chamber, and used their very daggers,
That they have done't?

48 **break**   give voice to
Have Macbeth and his wife already discussed the murder? In pairs, improvise a scene in which one person tries to persuade the other to do something that he/she does not want to do. Then reverse rôles.
50 **more . . .**   that is, king
51 **Nor . . . nor**   neither . . . nor
52 **adhere**   come together, suit, fit
   would make   wanted to arrange
53 **They**   that is, time and place
   made   arranged
   that their   their very
54 **unmake you**   takes away your courage
54–9 Do these lines show that Lady Macbeth is a merciless fiend (see Act V Scene 7 line 98), or does it prove the direct opposite? What do *you* think? Compare these lines with Macbeth's image of Pity on line 21 of this scene.
59 Some editions have Lady Macbeth saying 'We fail!' and some 'We fail.' Which of the three readings do you prefer, and why?
60 only screw up your courage firmly
   The image is taken from either (i) the tightening of a stringed musical instrument, until the peg is engaged to hold the string firm; or (ii) the winching of a crossbow until it is held tight by a notch ('sticking place') ready for firing
   Again, which image do you find more appropriate?
62 **the rather**   more than usual
63 **chamberlains**   servants of the bedchamber
64 **wassail**   literally, spiced ale; but Lady Macbeth may mean general merry-making
   convince   overpower
65 **warder**   guardian
66 **fume**   become blurred, as a gas
   the receipt of reason   the receptacle which holds reason (that is, the brain)
67 **limbec**   a distilling apparatus
68 **drenched**   drunken, drowned
71 **spongy**   sodden, full of liquid which has been soaked up like a sponge
72 **quell**   murder
73 **mettle**   spirit, courage, metal
74 **received**   accepted, believed

But screw your courage to the sticking place, And we'll not fail
Leicester Haymarket 1985

77 **other** otherwise
78 **As** since
   griefs . . . roar loud exclamations of anguish
79 What is it that makes Macbeth 'settled' and prepared to go ahead with the murder? Look back at his opening lines in this scene.
   bend up wind up (like a crossbow)
80 **corporal agent** part of my body
81 **mock . . . show** deceive everybody around by putting on the most happy of appearances
81-2 Where have we heard this kind of language used before?

In line 80, Macbeth describes what he and his wife are about to do as 'terrible'. Search through Act I and list all the examples you can which show that Macbeth is no morally blind psychopath, but that he knows the difference between right and wrong and yet cannot resist the idea of murder. Is this the way in which he can best be seen as tragic? Do you have any sympathy for him? Why – or why not?

Lady Macbeth   Who dares receive it other,
As we shall make our griefs and clamour roar
Upon his death?

Macbeth   I am settled, and bend up
Each corporal agent to this terrible feat.   80
Away, and mock the time with fairest show:
False face must hide what the false heart doth know.

[*Exeunt*]

Leicester Haymarket 1985

Act II

Scene 1

*Macbeth's castle. A courtyard. Enter **Banquo**, and **Fleance** with a torch before him.*

Banquo How goes the night, boy?

Fleance The moon is down; I have not heard the clock.

Banquo And she goes down at twelve.

Fleance   I take't, 'tis later, sir.

Banquo Hold, take my sword. There's husbandry in heaven,
Their candles are all out. Take thee that too.   5
A heavy summons lies like lead upon me,
And yet I would not sleep. Merciful powers,
Restrain in me the cursed thoughts that nature
Gives way to in repose! Give me my sword.
Who's there?   10

*[Enter **Macbeth**, and a **Servant** with a torch.]*

Macbeth A friend.

Banquo What, sir, not yet at rest? The king's a-bed.
He hath been in unusual pleasure, and
Sent forth great largess to your offices.
This diamond he greets your wife withal,   15
By the name of most kind hostess; and shut up
In measureless content.

Macbeth   Being unprepared,
Our will became the servant to defect,
Which else should free have wrought.

Banquo   All's well.
I dreamt last night of the three Weird Sisters: 20
To you they have showed some truth.

SD torch This may mean 'torch bearer'.
1 Banquo is asking about the time.
3 she that is, the moon (not the clock!)
4 husbandry economy, thrift
5 What does Banquo mean by heaven's 'candles'?
that What else do you suppose that Banquo gives Fleance to hold at this point?
6 summons call to sleep (see the final line of this scene)
7 would not don't want to
powers Banquo is referring to an order of angels who protect men from demons.
7–9 Shakespeare does not specify precisely what thoughts come to Banquo in sleep.
Is it a good idea to leave this to the audience's imagination? Pretend that you are Banquo and speak or write about your nightmares.
14 largess generous gifts
offices servants
15 withal with
16 By and calls her by
16–17 shut up ... content he has gone to bed utterly contented
17–19 Because we were unprepared for the King's visit we were not able to entertain him on as splendid a scale as we would have wished.

How long do you think has passed since the end of the previous scene? Would you have music between the scenes? If so, what kind? What mood would you wish to create?

In the Elizabethan Globe Theatre the whole play was acted in broad daylight. Find references on this page to ways in which Shakespeare indicates that the setting is a dark night.

Is Banquo troubled, on edge, even suspicious?

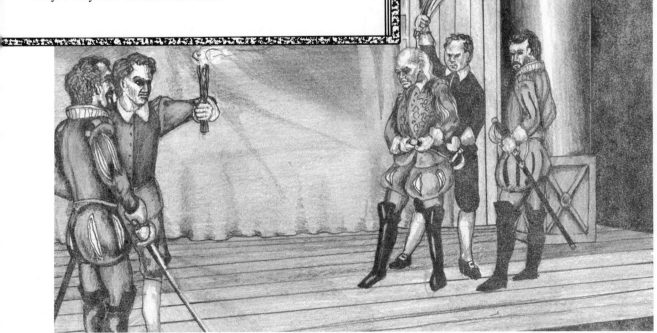

21   Macbeth's lie is breathtaking in its bluntness; and then he goes on to contradict himself.
22   **entreat . . . serve**   find a suitable opportunity
23   **would**   should
     Can you find any suggestion in this line that Macbeth is already thinking of himself as king?
25   **cleave . . . 'tis**   support me when the time comes
     Macbeth is deliberately ambiguous here: Is he referring to a natural death of Duncan and accession of himself? Or is he trying to bribe Banquo to support murder? Or, cleverly, is he allowing both meanings in order to sound out Banquo?
26–9   Banquo's reply makes it clear that he will do nothing dishonourable. From this moment Macbeth must recognise Banquo as an obstacle. Have you ever had moments when you know that somebody will never see things as you do? Compose a short dramatic script in which this happens.
26   **So**   so long as
     none   no honour
     Does Banquo mean honour in a different sense to that implied by Macbeth in the previous line?
27   **augment**   increase
28   my heart free from guilt and my loyalty untarnished
29   **be counselled**   take your advice
36–7   **sensible/To feeling**   able to be touched
37   **but**   only
39   **heat-oppressed**   feverish
40   **palpable**   touchable
41   **this**   Macbeth's own dagger
42   **marshall'st**   guide
     In which direction is the imaginary dagger pointing (or moving)?
44–5   **Mine eyes . . . rest**   Either my eyes are playing tricks, or my eyes are the only senses which are functioning normally.

Macbeth   I think not of them:
Yet, when we can entreat an hour to serve,
We would spend it in some words upon that business,
If you would grant the time.

Banquo   At your kind'st leisure.

Macbeth   If you shall cleave to my consent, when 'tis,   25
It shall make honour for you.

Banquo   So I lose none
In seeking to augment it, but still keep
My bosom franchised and allegiance clear,
I shall be counselled.

Macbeth   Good repose the while!

Banquo   Thanks, sir: the like to you!   30

[*Exeunt* **Banquo** *and* **Fleance**]

Macbeth   Go bid thy mistress, when my drink is ready,
She strike upon the bell. Get thee to bed.

[*Exit* **Servant**]

Is this a dagger which I see before me,
The handle toward my hand? Come, let me clutch thee.
I have thee not, and yet I see thee still.   35
Art thou not, fatal vision, sensible
To feeling as to sight? or art thou but
A dagger of the mind, a false creation,
Proceeding from the heat-oppressed brain?
I see thee yet, in form as palpable   40
As this which now I draw.
Thou marshall'st me the way that I was going,
And such an instrument I was to use!
Mine eyes are made the fools o'th'other senses,
Or else worth all the rest: I see thee still;   45

In Roman Polanski's 1972 film of *Macbeth* the dagger actually appears before Macbeth's eyes, a trick which is obviously not possible in the theatre. Is this a good idea? Should we see the dagger as well as Macbeth?

Banquo: **To you they have shown some truth**
Macbeth: **I think not of them**
RSC 1982

And on thy blade and dudgeon gouts of blood,
Which was not so before. There's no such thing:
It is the bloody business which informs
Thus to mine eyes. Now o'er the one half-world
Nature seems dead, and wicked dreams abuse   50
The curtained sleep; now witchcraft celebrates
Pale Hecate's off'rings; and withered Murder,
Alarumed by his sentinel, the wolf,
Whose howl's his watch, thus with his stealthy pace,
With Tarquin's ravishing strides, towards his design 55
Moves like a ghost. Thou sure and firm-set earth,
Hear not my steps, which way they walk, for fear
Thy very stones prate of my whereabout,
And take the present horror from the time,
Which now suits with it. Whiles I threat, he lives: 60
Words to the heat of deeds too cold breath gives.

[*A bell rings*]

I go, and it is done: the bell invites me.
Hear it not, Duncan, for it is a knell
That summons thee to heaven, or to hell.

[*Exit*]

Scene 2

Lady Macbeth *enters.*

Lady Macbeth   That which hath made them drunk hath made
    me bold:
What hath quenched them hath given me fire. Hark! Peace!
It was the owl that shrieked, the fatal bellman,
Which gives the stern'st good-night. He is about it:
The doors are open; and the surfeited grooms   5
Do mock their charge with snores: I have drugged their possets,
That death and nature do contend about them,
Whether they live or die.

46 **dudgeon** hilt, handle
    gouts thick drops
48 **inform** creates the form or shape
49 **half-world** hemisphere
50 **abuse** deceive
51 **curtained sleep** (i) eyelids; or (ii) the curtains
    drawn around a four-poster bed to exclude cold
    draughts
    There is an idea here of the violation of comfort and
    security.
52 **Pale Hecate's off'rings** offerings to Hecate, the
    goddess of witchcraft (who will appear later in the
    play) – she is 'Pale' because she is associated with
    the moon
52–6 Murder is personified as a withered creature (links
    with the witches?) creeping towards his victim.
53 **Alarumed** aroused, called to action
54 **Whose . . . watch** whose howl tells him the time
55 Tarquin was a rapist in ancient Rome. Notice that
    'ravishing' really refers to Tarquin, not his striding.
    This is called a 'transferred epithet'. Is it effective?
    design planned business (murder)
58 **prate** chatter
59 It is unclear what this line means – possibly: the
    noise will tell of my whereabouts and lessen the
    horrible silence of this time
60 **suits with it** is suitable for it
    threat threaten
61 He is saying that talking can become a substitute
    for action.
63 **knell** funeral bell

> In what mood does Macbeth end the
> scene?

1 She has been drinking.
2 The drink has put the attendants out (like a candle),
   but has 'set alight' Lady Macbeth and given her
   courage.
3 The owl was (and in some places still is)
   superstitiously considered a bird of ill-omen,
   heralding death.
   the fatal bellman (i) a man who visited a
   condemned man on the night before his execution;
   (ii) a man who walked before a dead body on its
   way to burial
4 **He is about it** Using information given during the
   rest of this scene, describe through the eyes of
   Macbeth what is happening off-stage.
5 **surfeited grooms** drunken servants
6 **Do . . . snores** neglect their duty by snoring
   possets bed-time drinks
7 **That** so that
   nature life

RSC 1986

11 **Confounds** ruins
12 **He . . . he** Macbeth . . . Duncan . . .
SD **Enter Macbeth** Write production notes (or tell somebody aloud) giving instructions to the actor playing Macbeth. How should he enter, walk, carry the daggers?
13 **My husband!** The only time in the play she calls him so. How does she say it? Experiment.
15 **crickets** also sometimes associated with death
15–21 What is the dramatic effect of all these short, breathless speeches?
22 **in's** in his
24 **addressed them** prepared themselves
25 She is probably referring to Malcolm and Donalbain, the King's sons, rather than to the two attendants.
27 **As** as if
hangman's hands A hangman sometimes had to draw and quarter his victim. 'Hangman' sometimes meant an executioner of any type.

Macbeth [*off-stage*]   Who's there? what, ho!

Lady Macbeth Alack! I am afraid they have awaked,
And 'tis not done: th'attempt and not the deed
Confounds us. Hark! I laid their daggers ready,
He could not miss 'em. Had he not resembled
My father as he slept, I had done't.

[*Enter* **Macbeth**]

My husband!

Macbeth I have done the deed. Didst thou not hear a noise?

Lady Macbeth I heard the owl scream, and the crickets cry.
Did you not speak?

Macbeth   When?

Lady Macbeth   Now.

Macbeth   As I descended?

Lady Macbeth Ay.

Macbeth Hark!
Who lies i'th' second chamber?

Lady Macbeth   Donalbain.

Macbeth This is a sorry sight.

Lady Macbeth A foolish thought, to say a sorry sight.

Macbeth There's one did laugh in's sleep, and one cried 'Murder!'
That they did wake each other: I stood and heard them:
But they did say their prayers, and addressed them
Again to sleep.

Lady Macbeth There are two lodged together.

Macbeth One cried 'God bless us!' and 'Amen' the other,
As they had seen me with these hangman's hands:

Consider it not so deeply.
RSC 1976

List'ning their fear, I could not say 'Amen',
When they did say 'God bless us'.

Lady Macbeth   Consider it not so deeply. 30

Macbeth   But wherefore could not I pronounce 'Amen'?
I had most need of blessing, and 'Amen'
Stuck in my throat.

Lady Macbeth   These deeds must not be thought
After these ways; so, it will make us mad.

Macbeth   Methought I heard a voice cry 'Sleep no more! 35
Macbeth does murder sleep', the innocent sleep,
Sleep that knits up the ravelled sleave of care,
The death of each day's life, sore labour's bath,
Balm of hurt minds, great Nature's second course,
Chief nourisher in life's feast, –

Lady Macbeth   What do you mean? 40

Macbeth   Still it cried 'Sleep no more!' to all the house:
'Glamis hath murdered sleep, and therefore Cawdor
Shall sleep no more: Macbeth shall sleep no more!'

Lady Macbeth   Who was it that thus cried? Why,
worthy thane,
You do unbend your noble strength, to think 45
So brainsickly of things. Go get some water,
And wash this filthy witness from your hand.
Why did you bring these daggers from the place?
They must lie there: go carry them, and smear
The sleepy grooms with blood. 50

Macbeth   I'll go no more:
I am afraid to think what I have done;
Look on't again I dare not.

Lady Macbeth   Infirm of purpose!
Give me the daggers: the sleeping and the dead
Are but as pictures: 'tis the eye of childhood
That fears a painted devil. If he do bleed, 55

28 **List'ning** listening to
31 **wherefore** why
33–4 Do these lines show that Lady Macbeth is self-controlled? Or that she is near to breaking point? How would you advise an actress to say them? Experiment with these lines, saying them in different ways into a tape recorder or to a partner.
35 **Methought** I thought, it seemed
37 Sleep which unravels the tangled skein (coil) of worry. The image is of a smoothing out of a confused mass of silken threads.
38 **sore labour's bath** as it were, a soothing bath after heavy labour
39 **second course** the main course of a meal
45 **unbend** loosen, slacken (see Act I Scene 7 line 79)
47 **witness** evidence
48 It is difficult to play this scene so that we may believe that Lady Macbeth has only just seen the daggers. Any suggestions?
50 **grooms** the king's bedroom attendants
52 **Infirm** weak
Where else does Lady Macbeth taunt her husband in this way?
53–4 In what way are the sleeping and the dead both like pictures?
55 **a painted devil** Brightly painted pictures of devils were used in some traditional stage performances.

Lines 35–43: Several Elizabethan poets had written on sleep as a gentle refuge from suffering. The voice – presumably of Macbeth's own imagination – suggests a fitting punishment for one who has violated the peace and security of sleep.
Write a poem entitled either 'Sleep' or 'Sleep no more!' It may, or may not, be about Macbeth.

Give me the daggers
Northcott Theatre 1986

56 gild Gold was often depicted as reddish in colour.
withal with it (Duncan's blood)

57 guilt Can you explain the pun here? Remember that when you hear the word in the theatre it would sound like 'gilt'. This is the kind of pun which the Elizabethans loved. Is it appropriate here at such a serious moment?

58 How is't what is the matter

59 In what sense do you think Macbeth sees his hands as plucking out his eyes? (See the Bible, Matthew 18:9.)

60 Neptune Roman god of the sea

61 rather instead

62 multitudinous great mass of
incarnadine make red

63 one totally

67–8 A little water . . . then! Compare with Act V Scene 1 line 38.

68–9 Your . . . unattended your firmness has deserted you

70 occasion call us something happens which causes us to be called (the knocking makes this highly likely)

71 watchers up and about, awake, not in bed

72 poorly weakly, wretchedly, helplessly

73 Critics interpret this line in various ways. What do *you* think that it means? Certainly, Macbeth does not want to face up to the responsibility of what he has done.

Write a speech for the council for the defence at Macbeth's trial for the murder of Duncan.

With detailed reference to the text, show how this scene creates a mood of suspense and horror.

I'll gild the faces of the grooms withal,
For it must seem their guilt.

[*She exits. Knocking within*]

Macbeth   Whence is that knocking?
How is't with me, when every noise appals me?
What hands are here? ha! they pluck out mine eyes!
Will all great Neptune's ocean wash this blood   60
Clean from my hand? No; this my hand will rather
The multitudinous seas incarnadine,
Making the green one red.

[**Lady Macbeth** *returns*]

Lady Macbeth My hands are of your colour; but I shame
To wear a heart so white. [*Knocking*] I hear a knocking   65
At the south entry: retire we to our chamber:
A little water clears us of this deed:
How easy it is then! Your constancy
Hath left you unattended. [*Knocking*] Hark! more knocking.
Get on your nightgown, lest occasion call us   70
And show us to be watchers: be not lost
So poorly in your thoughts.

Macbeth To know my deed, 'twere best not know myself.
[*Knocking*]
Wake Duncan with thy knocking! I would thou couldst!

[*Exeunt*]

My hands are of your colour
RSC 1976

Scene 3

Knocking within. Enter a **Porter.**

Porter   Here's a knocking indeed! If a man were porter of
hell-gate, he should have old turning the key. [*Knocking*]
Knock, knock, knock! Who's there, i'th' name of Beelzebub?
Here's a farmer, that hanged himself on th'expectation of
plenty: come in, time-server; have napkins enow about you;   5
here you'll sweat for't.   [*Knocking*] Knock, knock! Who's
there, in th'other devil's name? Faith, here's an equivocator,
that could swear in both the scales against either scale, who
committed treason enough for God's sake, yet could not
equivocate to heaven: O, come in, equivocator. [*Knocking*]   10
Knock, knock, knock! Who's there? Faith, here's an English
tailor come hither, for stealing out of a French hose: come in,
tailor, here you may roast your goose. [*Knocking*] Knock,
knock! never at quiet! What are you? But this place is too cold
for hell. I'll devil-porter it no further: I had thought to have   15
let in some of all professions, that go the primrose way to
th'everlasting bonfire. [*Knocking*] Anon, anon! I pray you,
remember the porter. [*Opens the gate*]

[Enter **Macduff** *and* **Lennox**]

Macduff   Was it so late, friend, ere you went to bed,
That you do lie so late?   20

Porter   Faith, sir, we were carousing till the second cock: and
drink, sir, is a great provoker of three things.

Macduff   What three things does drink especially provoke?

Porter   Marry, Sir, nose-painting, sleep, and urine.
Lechery, sir, it provokes and unprovokes: it provokes   25
the desire, but it takes away the performance. Therefore,
much drink may be said to be an equivocator with
lechery: it makes him, and it mars him; it sets him on,
and it takes him off; it persuades him, and disheartens
him; makes him stand to, and not stand to: in

SD   **Porter**   doorkeeper, gatekeeper
2   **hell-gate**   The Porter's joking pretence that he is the Porter of hell-gate is horribly appropriate in view of what has just happened (the fact that the Porter is unaware of this is called 'dramatic irony').
The Porter of hell-gate was a popular comic figure in medieval mystery plays.
old   much, plenty of
3   **Beelzebub**   the devil's lieutenant
4–18   The Porter imagines himself showing us round various inhabitants of hell.
4–5   **th'expectation of plenty**   A plentiful harvest would have brought down prices and ruined him.
5   **time-server**   This may mean here one who has served out a sentence (in this case, eternity!).
napkin's enow   enough handkerchiefs (to wipe off the sweat)
6   **for't**   for what you have done
7   **Faith**   a mild oath, short for 'In faith' (of God)
equivocator   one who pretends to tell the whole truth, but who deceives by ambiguous evasions
The play is full of equivocation. Who are the main equivocators in *Macbeth*?
8   **the scales**   of justice
Shakespeare may be referring to the trial of a Jesuit priest in 1606, who 'equivocated' when he gave evidence.
12   **French hose**   stockings or trousers in the French style
There were many jokes about tailors and they were often suspected of skimping on material and so cheating their customers.
13   **goose**   a tailor's pressing iron
16–17   **primrose ... bonfire**   the easy, pleasant path to hell
18   **remember ...**   he is thinking of a tip
21   **second cock**   second cock-crow (about 3 a.m.)
24   **Marry**   by the Virgin Mary
nose-painting   because boozing gives a red nose

It has been claimed that this episode with
the Porter is irrelevant, and was added later
by another playwright. What do you think?
Are there good dramatic reasons for its
inclusion?

How did you think that the part of the Porter
should be played? Does he talk directly to
the audience? Why does he speak in
prose?

Rewrite the Porter's speech for our times,
changing the types of people in hell and
adding comments as you think appropriate.

How would you costume the Porter?

RSC 1976

27-30 The Porter is saying that in various ways drink
       makes a man lustful but at the same time
       incapacitates him.
  30   **equivocates . . . sleep** (i) tricks him into falling
       asleep; (ii) deceives him in his sleep (because he
       has lustful dreams which have no reality)
30-1   **giving him the lie** (i) laying him out;
       (ii) deceiving him
33-5   The Porter willingly takes up the opportunity to pun,
       imagining that he fought his drunkenness like a
       wrestler.
  32   **i'the throat** a weak pun on telling a lie (there was
       an expression 'to lie in the throat', which meant to
       tell a big lie)
  33   **requited him** paid back the drink
  35   **made . . . cast him** managed to throw him off by
       (i) vomiting, or (ii) urinating
  40   **timely** early
  41   **slipped** missed
  44   **physics** cures
       Macbeth seems to affect a strained politeness
       when under stress.
  46   **limited service** appointed duty
  47   **He does . . . so** Is there a sign of guiltiness here
       which the audience, but not Lennox, can detect?

In lines 24–31 there is a series of antitheses
(look up 'antithesis' in a dictionary) which
amount to equivocation. Make a list of the
equivocations.

Do you think that this episode with the
Porter is a comic interlude or a deepening of
the atmosphere of evil? Or both?

---

conclusion, equivocates him in a sleep, and giving him   30
the lie, leaves him.

Macduff I believe drink gave thee the lie last night.

Porter That it did, sir, i'the very throat on me: but
I requited him for his lie, and, I think, being too strong
for him, though he took up my legs sometime, yet I
made a shift to cast him.   35

Macduff Is thy master stirring?

[*Enter* **Macbeth**]

Our knocking has awaked him; here he comes.

Lennox Good-morrow, noble sir.

Macbeth   Good-morrow, both.

Macduff Is the king stirring, worthy thane?

Macbeth   Not yet.

Macduff He did command me to call timely on him;   40
I have almost slipped the hour.

Macbeth   I'll bring you to him.

Macduff I know this is a joyful trouble to you;
But yet 'tis one.

Macbeth The labour we delight in physics pain.
This is the door.

Macduff   I'll make so bold to call,   45
For 'tis my limited service.

                                        [*Exit*]

Lennox Goes the king hence to-day?

Macbeth   He does: he did appoint so.

Lennox The night has been unruly: where we lay,
Our chimneys were blown down, and, as they say,

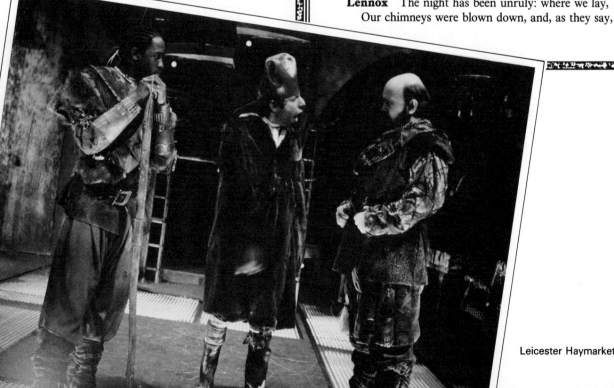

Leicester Haymarket 1985

Lamentings heard i'th'air, strange screams of death,   50
And prophesying with accents terrible
Of dire combustion and confused events
New hatched to th'woeful time. The obscure bird
Clamoured the livelong night: some say, the earth
Was feverous and did shake.

Macbeth   'Twas a rough night.   55

Lennox My young remembrance cannot parallel
A fellow to it.

[*Enter* **Macduff**]

Macduff O horror! horror! horror! Tongue, nor heart,
Cannot conceive nor name thee!

Macbeth, Lennox   What's the matter?

Macduff Confusion now hath made his masterpiece!   60
Most sacrilegious murder hath broke ope
The Lord's anointed temple, and stole thence
The life o'th'building.

Macbeth   What is't you say? the life?

Lennox Mean you his majesty?

Macduff Approach the chamber, and destroy your sight   65
With a new Gorgon: do not bid me speak;
See, and then speak yourselves.

[*Exeunt* **Macbeth** *and* **Lennox**]

                             Awake! awake!
Ring the alarum bell! Murder and treason!
Banquo and Donalbain! Malcolm! awake!
Shake off this downy sleep, death's counterfeit,   70
And look on death itself! up, up, and see
The great doom's image! Malcolm! Banquo!
As from your graves rise up, and walk like sprites,
To countenance this horror! Ring the bell. [*Bell rings*]

48-55 Macbeth's unnatural act is reflected by the wild weather. It is as if supernatural powers of evil have taken over, and the idea suggested by the Porter of Macbeth's castle as the gateway to hell is developed.

52 dire combustion terrible upheaval
There may be a reference here to the Gunpowder Plot.

53 to th'woeful time for this sad time
Why should Lennox speak like this? As far as he knows, all is well and successful in the state of Scotland.
   The obscure bird the owl (the bird of darkness)

54 livelong night whole night long

60 Confusion This was a strong word, meaning something like 'absolute chaos'.

61 ope open

62 The Lord's anointed temple A monarch was (and still is) anointed with holy oil at his or her coronation, and was supposed to rule by divine right authorised by God. The body of the monarch represented a temple of God (see the Bible, 1 Samuel 24:10 and 2 Corinthians 6:16). King James was keen to keep these ideas alive during his reign.

66 Gorgon In classical mythology, the Gorgons were sisters who were so hideously frightening to look at that all who did so were turned to stone.

70 downy soft and gentle (like down)
   counterfeit image, imitation

73 sprites spirits

74 countenance (i) face up to; (ii) be fitting for

67-74 One critic has visualised that in the Elizabethan theatre the scene may have appeared to an audience as follows:
'Standing probably . . . upon the upper stage, Macduff calls up "the sleepers of the house" to witness the "great doom's image", the Last Judgment. Rising in their nightshirts and flocking on to the stage by every entrance . . . they present a visual resemblance to the spirits rising from their graves on the Last Day, and the theatrical image complements the verbal image.'

75 **parley** a discussion between opposing forces during a truce, which was heralded by a trumpet In calling the alarm bell a trumpet Lady Macbeth reinforces the image of the Last Judgment.
76 **gentle lady** In what way is this dramatic irony?
78 **repetition** report
81 **Too cruel, anywhere** How should Banquo say this? Is he reproving Lady Macbeth; and, if so, why? Or is he lost in grief?
82 **prithee** pray you
84 **Had I but** if only I had
   chance happening, occurrence
86 **serious in mortality** worthwhile in human life
87 **toys** trifles
88-9 Wine may be red, and so the image is of wine being drained like Duncan's blood, so that only the dregs ('lees') remain. 'Vault' means 'earth', with the sky overhead – in the Elizabethan theatre the roof over the stage represented the sky and heaven. 'Vault' also continues the wine image, wine (particularly the best) being stored in a cellar or vault.
84-9 What Macbeth says is all true. Is he unconscious of the irony, or is he merely being a hypocrite? Compare with Act V Scene 5 line 19–28.
90 **amiss** wrong

The underside of the roof of the stage would have been decorated like this in the Globe Theatre.

[*Enter* **Lady Macbeth**]

Lady Macbeth   What's the business,
That such a hideous trumpet calls to parley   75
The sleepers of the house? speak, speak!

Macduff   O, gentle lady,
'Tis not for you to hear what I can speak:
The repetition, in a woman's ear,
Would murder as it fell.

[*Enter* **Banquo**]

                         O Banquo! Banquo!
Our royal master's murdered!

Lady Macbeth   Woe, alas!   80
What, in our house?

Banquo   Too cruel, anywhere.
Dear Duff, I prithee, contradict thyself,
And say it is not so.

[**Macbeth** *and* **Lennox** *return*]

Macbeth   Had I but died an hour before this chance,
I had lived a blessed time; for from this instant   85
There's nothing serious in mortality;
All is but toys: renown and grace is dead,
The wine of life is drawn, and the mere lees
Is left this vault to brag of.

[*Enter* **Malcolm** *and* **Donalbain**]

Donalbain   What is amiss?

Macbeth   You are, and do not know't: 90
The spring, the head, the fountain of your blood
Is stopped – the very source of it is stopped.

Macduff   Your royal father's murdered.

Malcolm   O, by whom?

Lennox   Those of his chamber, as it seemed, had done't:
Their hands and faces were all badged with blood,   **95**
So were their daggers, which unwiped we found
Upon their pillows: they stared, and were distracted;
No man's life was to be trusted with them.

Macbeth   O, yet I do repent me of my fury,
That I did kill them.

Macduff   Wherefore did you so?   **100**

Macbeth   Who can be wise, amazed, temp'rate and furious,
Loyal and neutral, in a moment? no man:
Th'expedition of my violent love
Outrun the pauser, reason. Here lay Duncan,
His silver skin laced with his golden blood,   **105**
And his gashed stabs looked like a breach in nature
For ruin's wasteful entrance: there, the murderers,
Steeped in the colours of their trade, their daggers
Unmannerly breeched with gore: who could refrain,
That had a heart to love, and in that heart   **110**
Courage to make's love known?

Lady Macbeth   [*Fainting*]   Help me hence, ho!

Macduff   Look to the lady.

Malcolm   [*Aside to* **Donalbain**]   Why do we hold our
    tongues,
That most may claim this argument for ours?

Donalbain   [*Aside to* **Malcolm**]   What should be
    spoken here, where our fate,
Hid in an auger-hole, may rush and seize us?   **115**
Let's away.
Our tears are not yet brewed.

Malcolm   [*Aside to* **Donalbain**]   Nor our strong sorrow
Upon the foot of motion.

Banquo   Look to the lady.

---

95 badged   marked, indicating what they are
        (murderers) as if by a badge
100 What do you think is going on in Macduff's mind?
101 amazed   The word had a very strong meaning in
        Shakespeare's day – almost 'demented'.
103 expedition   haste
104 pauser   that which causes delay
        Macbeth is saying that he acted quickly without
        pause for thought.
105 Shakespeare makes something horrible sound
        beautiful. This may be done in order to show up
        Macbeth's words as rather artificial.
        laced   interlaced, criss-crossed
        golden   see note on Act II Scene 2 line 56
106–7 breach . . . entrance   The openings of Duncan's
        wound look like the breach in a wall through which
        attackers enter and lay waste the town. The
        unnaturalness of the act is emphasised.
109 Unmannerly . . . gore   dressed in blood up to the
        hilt after their improper assault on Duncan
        'Breeched' is suggested by line 106, and the image
        of trousers on daggers is ridiculous and the kind of
        language at which Shakespeare often poked fun.
        Why, then, does he use this image?
111 make's   make his
        Does Lady Macbeth really faint, or is she
        pretending? Think of reasons for each possibility.
112 to   after
113 argument   subject, theme
114 should be spoken   can be said
115 auger-hole   a very small hole made by a
        carpentry instrument
        Donalbain is suggesting that a similar fate to their
        father's may be lurking and waiting for them in an
        unsuspected place.
117– Malcolm is saying that they feel great sorrow but
  18 are not ready to express it. He is probably uneasy
        at Macbeth's public expressions of grief.

**Who can be wise, amazed, temp'rate and
    furious,
Loyal and neutral, in a moment?**

RSC 1974

119 **naked frailties hid** These words could have
    several levels of meaning, not all of which may be
    consciously intended by Banquo. Discuss this. How
    does this apply to all on stage? How to Malcolm
    and Donalbain? How to Macbeth and Lady
    Macbeth?
121 **question** examine, discuss
122 **scruples** doubts, suspicions
124 **undivulged pretence** secret plots
125 **Of** against
126 **briefly** quickly
    manly readiness either (i) suitable masculine
    clothes (instead of night-shirts), or (ii) a
    preparedness for action as befits men
128 **consort** associate
129– See note to lines 117–18. Do they already
 30 suspect Macbeth?
129 **office** function, duty
133 **near** nearer
    He is saying that the closer one is in relationship to
    the murdered man, the more danger one is in.
134 **shaft** arrow
135 **lighted** reached its ultimate target
137 **dainty of** particular in, ceremonious in
138 **shift away** slip away
    warrant justification
138–9 **that theft . . . itself** a pun on 'steal away'
    meaning 'creep away quietly'
    Shakespeare uses this pun in at least two other
    plays.

Write or improvise a scene in which they all
'meet i'th'hall together' (see line 127). Is it at
this point that Macbeth is elected king?
There is no need to attempt to reproduce
Shakespearean language.

While Macbeth is on stage during this scene
the audience are aware of how different his
thoughts are from his words. On the
evidence of his words and deeds, what
would you suggest were his thoughts? You
could write or speak as if you were Macbeth.

Discuss how Macbeth handles the discovery
of Duncan's murder.

And when we have our naked frailties hid,
That suffer in exposure, let us meet,   120
And question this most bloody piece of work,
To know it further. Fears and scruples shake us:
In the great hand of God I stand, and thence
Against the undivulged pretence I fight
Of treasonous malice.

Macduff   And so do I.

All   So all.   125

Macbeth Let's briefly put on manly readiness.
And meet i'th'hall together.

All   Well contented.

[Exeunt all but **Malcolm** *and* **Donalbain**]

Malcolm What will you do? Let's not consort with them:
To show an unfelt sorrow is an office
Which the false man does easy. I'll to England.   130

Donalbain To Ireland, I: our separated fortune
Shall keep us both the safer: where we are
There's daggers in men's smiles: the near in blood,
The nearer bloody.

Malcolm   This murderous shaft that's shot
Hath not yet lighted, and our safest way   135
Is to avoid the aim. Therefore to horse,
And let us not be dainty of leave-taking,
But shift away: there's warrant in that theft
Which steals itself when there's no mercy left.

[Exeunt]

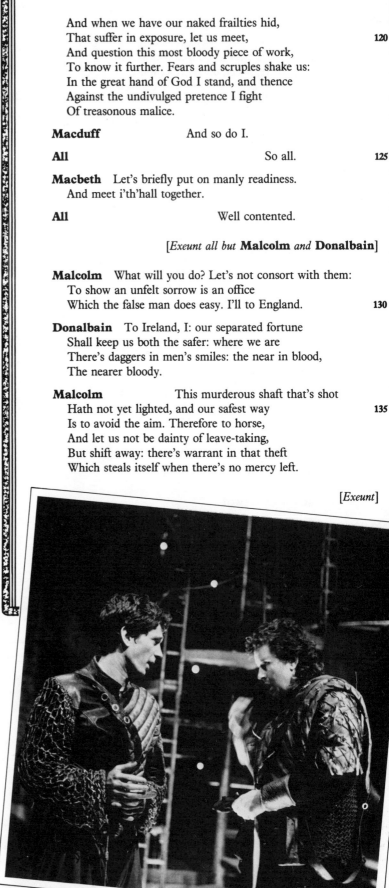

**What will you do? Let's not consort with
them:**
Leicester Haymarket 1985

Scene 4

Outside Macbeth's castle. Enter **Ross** *with an* **Old Man.**

Old Man Threescore and ten I can remember well,
Within the volume of which time I have seen
Hours dreadful and things strange; but this sore night
Hath trifled former knowings.

Ross   Ha, good father,
Thou seest the heavens, as troubled with man's act,   5
Threatens his bloody stage: by th' clock 'tis day,
And yet dark night strangles the travelling lamp:
Is't night's predominance, or the day's shame,
That darkness does the face of earth entomb,
When living light should kiss it?

Old Man   'Tis unnatural,   10
Even like the deed that's done. On Tuesday last
A falcon towering in her pride of place
Was by a mousing owl hawked at and killed.

Ross And Duncan's horses – a thing most strange and
  certain –
Beauteous and swift, the minions of their race,   15
Turned wild in nature, broke their stalls, flung out,
Contending 'gainst obedience, as they would make
War with mankind.

Old Man   'Tis said they ate each other.

Ross They did so, to th'amazement of mine eyes,
That looked upon't.

[*Enter* **Macduff**]

                    Here comes the good Macduff.   20
How goes the world, sir, now?

Macduff   Why, see you not?

1   How old is the Old Man?
3   **sore** terrible
4   **trifled former knowings** made my previous
    experiences seem trivial
5   **as** as if
5–6 There are three words in these lines that have a
    theatrical sense.
6   **his bloody stage** that is, the earth upon which
    man does bloody deeds
    by th' according to the
7   **travelling lamp** sun
8–10 Ross is wondering whether the powers of darkness
    (and evil) have overpowered day, or whether the
    day is ashamed to shed light on the deed that has
    happened at night.
10–20 It was a common idea that unnatural and evil
    deeds are reflected in nature. Discuss how this idea
    is used in films, particularly horror films. Write a
    short piece of screenplay which demonstrates this
    idea.
12 **towering . . . place** circling upwards to her
    highest point (before swooping on her prey)
    These are terms from falconry, the most popular
    Elizabethan gentleman's sport. Shakespeare uses
    many such terms in his plays.
13 A falcon is a much more powerful kind of hawk
    than an owl, which normally hunts mice. This shows
    another reversal of the natural order of things.
15 **minions** favourites
    race breed
16 **Turned wild in nature** reverted to their wild
    state
    flung lashed
17 **Contending 'gainst obedience** fighting against
    (human) control
    as as if

Re-read carefully lines 1–20 (**. . . looked
upon't**). How do you think this exchange
contributes to the effect of the play?

With close reference to other parts of the
play, show how an impression of unnatural
happenings is developed during *Macbeth*.

. . . night strangles the travelling lamp
Engraving from R Fludd, *Utriusque Cosmi Metaphysica*, 1617

24 **good** advantage
  pretend hope for
  suborned encouraged (to do it), bribed
26 See Act II Scene 3 line 138–9.
27–9 As Ross implies, there could hardly be a more
  unnatural deed than killing the father who gave you
  life.
28 **Thriftless** wasteful, destructive
  ravin up ravenously devour
31 **named** chosen
  Scone the place where Scottish kings were
  crowned on the Stone of Destiny
  The Stone still exists. Find out where it is.
32 **invested** crowned as king, and clothed in a
  monarch's robes
33 **Colmekill** Iona, the holy island where Scottish
  kings were buried
36 **Fife** Macduff's home territory
38 Another clothing image suggesting that the new
  times will be less good than the old.
40 **benison** blessing

Examine this scene closely, and contrast the
attitudes of the three characters in the
scene. Is Ross straightforward and rather
credulous? Is Macduff more suspicious,
even sarcastic (line 38)? Is the Old Man
sincere in lines 40–1, or does he see Ross as
one who will serve whoever happens to be
in power?

What is the dramatic purpose of this scene?

**Well, may you see things well done there:
adieu!**
Leicester Haymarket 1985

Ross   Is't known who did this more than bloody deed?

Macduff   Those that Macbeth hath slain.

Ross   Alas, the day!
What good could they pretend?

Macduff   They were suborned.
Malcolm and Donalbain, the king's two sons,   25
Are stol'n away and fled, which puts upon them
Suspicion of the deed.

Ross   'Gainst nature still!
Thriftless ambition, that wilt ravin up
Thine own life's means! Then 'tis most like
The sovereignty will fall upon Macbeth.   30

Macduff   He is already named, and gone to Scone
To be invested.

Ross   Where is Duncan's body?

Macduff   Carried to Colmekill,
The sacred storehouse of his predecessors,
And guardian of their bones.   35

Ross   Will you to Scone?

Macduff   No cousin, I'll to Fife.

Ross   Well, I will thither.

Macduff   Well, may you see things well done there: adieu!
Lest our old robes sit easier than our new!

Ross   Farewell, father.

Old Man   God's benison go with you, and with those   40
That would make good of bad and friends of foes!

                                                    [*Exeunt*]

Act III

Scene 1

The palace at Forres. **Banquo** *enters.*

Banquo   Thou hast it now, King, Cawdor, Glamis, all,
As the weird women promised, and I fear
Thou play'dst most foully for't: yet it was said
It should not stand in thy posterity,
But that myself should be the root and father   5
Of many kings. If there come truth from them –
As upon thee, Macbeth their speeches shine –
Why, by the verities on thee made good,
May they not be my oracles as well,
And set me up in hope? But hush, no more.   10

[*Sennet sounded. Enter* **Macbeth**, *as King,* **Lady Macbeth**, *as Queen,* **Lennox**, **Ross**, **Lords**, **Ladies** *and* **Attendants**]

Macbeth   Here's our chief guest.

Lady Macbeth   If he had been forgotten,
It had been as a gap in our great feast,
And all-thing unbecoming.

Macbeth   To-night we hold a solemn supper, sir,
And I'll request your presence.   15

Banquo   Let your highness
Command upon me, to the which my duties
Are with a most indissoluble tie
For ever knit.

Macbeth   Ride you this afternoon?

Banquo   Ay, my good lord.

4 that the kingdom should not be passed on to your children
5 **root and father** The image is that of a 'family tree', which shows the branches of a family growing from a root.
8 **verities** truths
9 **oracles** prophets
SD **Sennet** a series of notes played on a trumpet which herald the arrival of an important person
13 **all-thing** totally, wholly
14 **solemn** formal, ceremonial (not 'serious' in the modern sense)
16 **the which** that is, your command
19 The reason for this question, and for those on lines 23 and 35, will soon become apparent. Does the whole court hear this conversation? Or is it a private one between Macbeth and Banquo? If private, what is Lady Macbeth doing?

Is Banquo an accessory after the fact of murder? Write a short report to send to Macduff at Fife assessing Banquo's part in the affair up to this point in time.

The historical Banquo helped Macbeth to kill Duncan. Why do you think that Shakespeare changed Banquo's rôle in his drama?

Write a few director's notes to be given to the main actors in this scene (up to line 43). Follow this up with a workshop rehearsal.

I fear
Thou play'dst most foully for't
Great Eastern Stage 1985

21 **still** always
   grave and prosperous weighty and profitable
22 **take** take your advice
25 **Go not ... better** unless my horse travels faster
   than I expect him to
29 **bestowed** settled
32 **invention** lies. What lies?
33 **therewithal** besides that
   cause affairs
34 **Craving us jointly** demanding the attention of
   both of us
   Hie hurry
36 **our time does call upon's** it's time for us to get
   going
41 **society** company
43 **while** until
   This usage is still common in areas of the north-east
   of England.
44 **Sirrah** a form of address to an inferior
46 **without** outside

Macbeth   We should have else desired your good advice   20
Which still hath been both grave and prosperous
In this day's council; but we'll take to-morrow.
Is't far you ride?

Banquo   As far, my lord, as will fill up the time
'Twixt this and supper. Go not my horse the better,   25
I must become a borrower of the night
For a dark hour or twain.

Macbeth   Fail not our feast.

Banquo   My lord, I will not.

Macbeth   We hear our bloody cousins are bestowed
In England and in Ireland, not confessing   30
Their cruel parricide, filling their hearers
With strange invention: but of that to-morrow,
When therewithal we shall have cause of state
Craving us jointly. Hie you to horse: adieu,
Till you return at night. Goes Fleance with you?   35

Banquo   Ay, my good lord: our time does call upon's.

Macbeth   I wish your horses swift and sure of foot:
And so I do commend you to their backs.
Farewell.

[*Exit* **Banquo**]

Let every man be master of his time   40
Till seven at night; to make society
The sweeter welcome, we will keep ourself
Till supper-time alone: while then, God be with you!

[*All depart but* **Macbeth** *and a* **Servant**]

Sirrah, a word with you: attend those men
Our pleasure?   45

Servant   They are, my lord, without the palace gate.

Young Vic 1984

Macbeth   Bring them before us.

[*The **Servant** goes*]

To be thus is nothing,
But to be safely thus: our fears in Banquo
Stick deep, and in his royalty of nature
Reigns that which would be feared. 'Tis much he dares,   50
And, to that dauntless temper of his mind,
He hath a wisdom that doth guide his valour
To act in safety. There is none but he
Whose being I do fear: and under him
My Genius is rebuked, as it is said   55
Mark Antony's was by Caesar. He chid the Sisters,
When first they put the name of king upon me,
And bade them speak to him; then prophet-like
They hailed him father to a line of kings:
Upon my head they placed a fruitless crown,   60
And put a barren sceptre in my gripe,
Thence to be wrenched with an unlineal hand,
No son of mine succeeding. If't be so,
For Banquo's issue have I filed my mind,
For them the gracious Duncan have I murdered,   65
Put rancours in the vessel of my peace
Only for them, and mine eternal jewel
Given to the common enemy of man,
To make them kings, the seed of Banquo kings!
Rather than so, come Fate into the list,   70
And champion me to th'utterance. Who's there?

[*Re-enter the **Servant** with two **Murderers***]

Now go to the door, and stay there till we call.

[*Exit **Servant***]

Was it not yesterday we spoke together?

47   **thus**   that is, king
48   **But to be**   unless one can be
      in   of
49   **Stick deep**   like thorns
      royalty of nature   Macbeth sees Banquo's natural
      nobility.
50   **Reigns**   Why does Shakespeare choose this word?
      would   must
51   **to**   in addition to
      temper   character
54   **being**   existence
55   **My Genius is rebuked**   my spirit is made to feel
      inferior
      It was an old idea that one man's guardian spirit
      might overcome another, leading to a fall in the first
      man's fortunes.
56   **Caesar**   Octavius Caesar
      Shakespeare wrote about this in *Antony and Cleopatra*
      (see Act II Scene 3 of that play).
      chid   challenged
60-1   **fruitless ... barren ...**   because (according to the
      witches) no descendant of his will inherit the crown
      Lady Macbeth has told us that she has 'given suck',
      but we gain an impression that, as was common in
      those days, her children have died in infancy.
61   **gripe**   grip, grasp
62   **with an unlineal hand**   by one not descended
      from me
64   **issue**   off-spring, descendants
      filed   defiled
65   **gracious Duncan**   What is Macbeth's attitude
      towards the man he has murdered?
66   put bitterness in the calm of my mind
      Macbeth uses the image of a drinking vessel into
      which 'rancours' (bitter pieces in food or drink) have
      been dropped.
67   **mine eternal jewel**   my soul
68   **the common enemy of man**   the devil, Satan
70-1   Rather than give in to such an idea, Macbeth
      challenges Fate itself to enter the lists (a place
      where tournaments of jousting took place) and fight
      against ('champion') him to the death ('to
      th'utterance' means to the ultimate conclusion –
      that is, death).

> Rewrite lines 56 **(He chid ...)** to 71 in good modern English.

To be thus is nothing
RSC 1986

76 he...which... Banquo...who...
77 under fortune beneath what you deserve
78 made good explained
79 passed...you proved to you
80 borne in hand deceived
   crossed thwarted, done down
   instruments means by which these things were
   done
81 wrought with them was behind these things
82 half a soul a half-wit
   notion mind
85 Our point of the point of our
87 so gospelled such Christians
90 yours your families
   What does the 1st Murderer imply in his answer to
   Macbeth?
91 go pass
92-3 hounds...demi-wolves various breeds of dog
93 clept called
94 valued file catalogue listing values and qualities
96 housekeeper watchdog
98 closed enclosed, placed
99 Particular addition individual description
   bill list
100 writes...alike that is, merely lists them all as
   'dog'
101 station position, place
   file (i) as in line 94; (ii) as in a military rank
**101-5 station...file...rank...enemy...
   grapples...** To what image of themselves is
   Macbeth appealing here?
102 say't say so
103 bosoms hearts, minds
104 takes...off removes (by death)
105 Grapples you binds you tightly
   us the royal plural

Compare the methods used by Macbeth to
urge on the murderers with those used
earlier by Lady Macbeth to push Macbeth
himself towards murder.

Ay, in the catalogue ye go for men
Leicester Haymarket 1985

1st Murderer   It was, so please your highness.

Macbeth   Well then, now
    Have you considered of my speeches? Know   75
    That it was he in the times past which held you
    So under fortune, which you thought had been
    Our innocent self: this I made good to you
    In our last conference; passed in probation with you,
    How you were borne in hand, how crossed, the instruments, 80
    Who wrought with them, and all things else that might
    To half a soul and to a notion crazed
    Say 'Thus did Banquo'.

1st Murderer   You made it known to us.

Macbeth   I did so; and went further, which is now
    Our point of second meeting. Do you find   85
    Your patience so predominant in your nature,
    That you can let this go? Are you so gospelled,
    To pray for this good man, and for his issue,
    Whose heavy hand hath bowed you to the grave
    And beggared yours for ever?

1st Murderer   We are men, my liege. 90

Macbeth   Ay, in the catalogue ye go for men,
    As hounds and greyhounds, mongrels, spaniels, curs,
    Shoughs, water-rugs, and demi-wolves, are clept
    All by the name of dogs: the valued file
    Distinguishes the swift, the slow, the subtle,   95
    The housekeeper, the hunter, every one
    According to the gift which bounteous nature
    Hath in him closed, whereby he does receive
    Particular addition, from the bill
    That writes them all alike: and so of men.   100
    Now, if you have a station in the file,
    Not i'th' worst rank of manhood, say't,
    And I will put that business in your bosoms,
    Whose execution takes your enemy off,
    Grapples you to the heart and love of us   105

Who wear our health but sickly in his life,
Which in his death were perfect.

2nd Murderer   I am one, my liege.
Whom the vile blows and buffets of the world
Hath so incensed that I am reckless what
I do to spite the world.

1st Murderer   And I another   110
So weary with disasters, tugged with fortune,
That I would set my life on any chance,
To mend it, or be rid on't.

Macbeth   Both of you
Know Banquo was your enemy.

Both Murderers   True, my lord.

Macbeth   So is he mine: and in such bloody distance,   115
That every minute of his being thrusts
Against my near'st of life: and though I could
With barefaced power sweep him from my sight,
And bid my will avouch it, yet I must not,
For certain friends that are both his and mine,   120
Whose loves I may not drop, but wail his fall
Who I myself struck down: and thence it is
That I to your assistance do make love,
Masking the business from the common eye,
For sundry weighty reasons.   125

2nd Murderer   We shall, my lord,
Perform what you command us.

1st Murderer   Though our lives –

Macbeth   Your spirits shine through you. Within this hour at
     most
I will advise you where to plant yourselves,
Acquaint you with the perfect spy o'th' time,
The moment on't, for't must be done to-night,   130
And something from the palace; always thought
That I require a clearness: and with him –

106–7 Macbeth is saying that while Banquo lives his (Macbeth's) health is poor, but it will be perfect when Banquo is dead.
111 tugged with pulled about by (as in wrestling)
112 set risk, stake
113 to improve my life or be free of it
115 bloody distance deadly closeness (an image from fencing, which is developed in the following two lines)
116 being life, existence
117 near'st of life the most vital part of my body
118 barefaced open and unashamed
119 bid . . . it justify it as merely my wish (that is, openly behave like a tyrant and publicly do what I wish)
120 For because of
121 wail must (publicly) show sorrow for
125 sundry various
126 What do you think that the 1st Murderer is about to say?
127 Your spirits . . . you Does Macbeth intend irony here?
129 perfect spy o'th'time precise information as to the right time (for the deed)
131 something some distance
    thought bearing in mind
132 clearness freedom from suspicion
    him Banquo

Spot the clothing imagery on this page.

Both of you
Know Banquo was your enemy
Leicester Haymarket 1985

133 **rubs or botches** mistakes or bunglings ('botching' was poor repair work, and often referred to mended clothes)
135 **absence** that is, death
      material important
137 **Resolve yourself apart** stand aside, discuss it between yourselves, and make up your minds
139 **call . . . straight** need you immediately

1 Does Lady Macbeth suspect that her husband may be plotting against Banquo? If so, give evidence.
4–7 Compare with her words in Act I Scene 5 lines 68–9. What effect does Shakespeare create by making these lines rhyme?
4 **had** gained
7 **doubtful** fearful, apprehensive, insecure

To leave no rubs nor botches in the work –
Fleance his son, that keeps him company,
Whose absence is no less material to me   135
Than is his father's, must embrace the fate
Of that dark hour. Resolve yourselves apart;
I'll come to you anon.

Both Murderers   We are resolved, my lord.

Macbeth   I'll call upon you straight; abide within.

> [*Exeunt* **Murderers**]

It is concluded: Banquo, thy soul's flight,
If it find heaven, must find it out to-night.

> [*Exit*]

Scene 2

Enter **Lady Macbeth** *and a* **Servant**.

Lady Macbeth   Is Banquo gone from court?

Servant   Ay, madam, but returns again to-night.

Lady Macbeth   Say to the king, I would attend his leisure
For a few words.

Servant   Madam, I will.

> [*He goes*]

Lady Macbeth   Nought's had, all's spent,
Where our desire is got without content: 5
'Tis safer to be that which we destroy
Than by destruction dwell in doubtful joy.

> [*Enter* **Macbeth**]

How now, my lord! why do you keep along,

> Compare Macbeth's preparation for murdering Banquo with that before the murder of Duncan.

. . . without content

Top to bottom: Leicester Haymarket 1985, National Theatre Workshop 1978, RSC 1986

Of sorriest fancies your companions making,
Using those thoughts which should indeed have died   10
With them they think on? Things without all remedy
Should be without regard: what's done, is done.

Macbeth   We have scotched the snake, not killed it:
She'll close and be herself, whilst our poor malice
Remains in danger of her former tooth.   15
But let the frame of things disjoint, both the worlds suffer,
Ere we will eat our meal in fear and sleep
In the affliction of these terrible dreams
That shake us nightly: better be with the dead,
Whom we, to gain our peace, have sent to peace,   20
Than on the torture of the mind to lie
In restless ecstasy. Duncan is in his grave;
After life's fitful fever he sleeps well;
Treason has done his worst: nor steel, nor poison,
Malice domestic, foreign levy, nothing,   25
Can touch him further.

Lady Macbeth   Come on;
Gentle my lord, sleek o'er your rugged looks,
Be bright and jovial among your guests to-night.

Macbeth   So shall I, love, and so I pray be you:
Let your remembrance apply to Banquo;   30
Present him eminence, both with eye and tongue:
Unsafe the while, that we
Must lave our honours in these flattering streams,
And make our faces vizards to our hearts,
Disguising what they are.

Lady Macbeth   You must leave this.   35

Macbeth   O, full of scorpions is my mind, dear wife!
Thou know'st that Banquo and his Fleance lives.

Lady Macbeth   But in them nature's copy's not eterne.

Macbeth   There's comfort yet; they are assailable,
Then be thou jocund: ere the bat hath flown   40

9   sorriest   most miserable
10   Using   keeping company with
11   without   beyond
12   without regard   beyond thinking about, not
thought about at all
what's done, is done   see Act V Scene 1 lines
59–60
13   scotched   slashed, wounded
14   close   heal
poor   weak
15   her former tooth   the strength of her fangs before
she was wounded
16   but let the universe collapse, heaven and earth
being destroyed
17   Ere   before
19–26   He amplifies what Lady Macbeth has just said.
20   peace . . . peace   peace of mind which we
expected the fulfilment of ambition to bring . . . the
peace of death
21   The metaphor is of the rack, a common form of
torture.
22   ecstasy   delirium, mental turmoil
25   Malice . . . levy   civil war, troops from abroad (as
at the beginning of the play)
27   Gentle my   This kind of reversal of words is
common in Elizabethan English.
sleek o'er   smooth down (as hair)
30   Be especially attentive to Banquo.
Why does Macbeth say this to his wife, when he
hopes that Banquo will by then be dead?
31   pay him high honour and respect
32   Unsafe the while, that   while we are insecure
33   must wash (and so give a clean appearance) our
honour in streams of flattery (by being courteous to
Banquo)
34   vizards   (i) masks; (ii) steel face-guards on
helmets of the time
Both made it impossible to see the expression on
the face of the wearer.
35   leave   stop thinking like
38   nature's copy's not eterne   (i) although made in
nature's (God's) image, they are not immortal;
(ii) nature has not given them an eternal lease
('copy' = copyhold or leasehold) of life
39   There's   in that fact there is
40   jocund   joyful

A critic has said that in this scene (and
others) we see Macbeth and Lady Macbeth
suffering the torments of the damned. What
indications have you found in the play that
Macbeth's castle represents hell?

Look again at lines 10–35, and comment in
detail on anything there which is connected
with other events in the play.

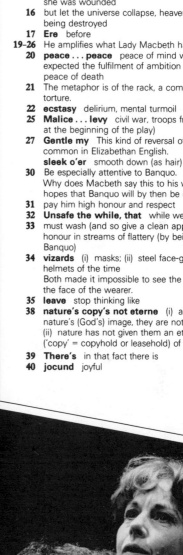

Gentle my lord; sleek o'er your rugged looks

Oxford Playhouse 1982

41   **cloistered**   (i) among cloisters; (ii) dark
     Hecate   Compare with Act II Scene 1 line 52.
     Note that she is now described as 'black'
     [= (i) dark; (ii) evil].
42   **shard-borne**   (i) born in dung; (ii) carried on scaly
     wings
43   **yawning peal**   curfew bell which announces that
     it is time for sleep
45   **chuck**   a common term of endearment
     Is it inappropriate that Macbeth should use it here?
46   **seeling**   blinding, eye-closing
     The eyelids of falcons were stitched up during
     training.
47   **Scarf up**   blindfold
     A scarf was a leather hood placed over a falcon's
     head, and was another way of blinding it during
     training.
49   **bond**   moral law against killing – the word has
     legal overtones.
50   **thickens**   dims
51   **rooky**   black and full of rooks
54   **hold thee still**   do not be anxious
55   **ill**   evil, worse

SD   Macbeth has sent another thug to check on the
     first two. What does this emphasise about his state
     of mind?
2   **He ... mistrust**   we need not mistrust him
3   **offices**   instructions
4   **To ... just**   exactly as we were previously directed
6   **lated**   belated
     apace   quickly
7   **To ... inn**   to reach the inn in good time
8   **The ... watch**   that is, Banquo

Examine Scene 2 carefully, and then say in
what ways you detect the beginnings of a
reversal in the rôles of Macbeth and Lady
Macbeth. Is the relationship between them
changing? Quote evidence to prove your
points.

What would be lost if this scene were cut
from the play?

One critic has called Lady Macbeth 'the
perfect wife'. How far do you agree with this
verdict?

Write down accurately lines 46–56 (from
Come, seeling night...). Learn them.
Write them out from memory (punctuation
does not matter). Recite them from
memory. Compare the way you say the lines
with the way somebody else interprets
them. How is Shakespeare encouraging his
audience to use their imagination in these
lines?

Discuss how the language and imagery
creates a mood (a) in these lines, and (b) in
the play as a whole.

His cloistered flight, ere to black Hecate's summons
The shard-borne beetle with his drowsy hums
Hath rung night's yawning peal, there shall be done
A deed of dreadful note.

Lady Macbeth   What's to be done?

Macbeth   Be innocent of the knowledge, dearest chuck,   45
Till thou applaud the deed. Come, seeling night,
Scarf up the tender eye of pitiful day,
And with thy bloody and invisible hand
Cancel and tear to pieces that great bond
Which keeps me pale! Light thickens, and the crow   50
Makes wing to th' rooky wood:
Good things of day begin to droop and drowse,
Whiles night's black agents to their preys do rouse.
Thou marvell'st at my words: but hold thee still;
Things bad begun make strong themselves by ill: 55
So, prithee, go with me.

                                   [*Exeunt*]

Scene 3

A park, with a road leading to the palace. Enter three
Murderers.

1st Murderer   But who did bid thee join with us?

3rd Murderer   Macbeth.

2nd Murderer   He needs not our mistrust, since he delivers
Our offices and what we have to do,
To the direction just.

1st Murderer   Then stand with us.
The west yet glimmers with some streaks of day: 5
Now spurs the lated traveller apace
To gain the timely inn, and near approaches
The subject of our watch.

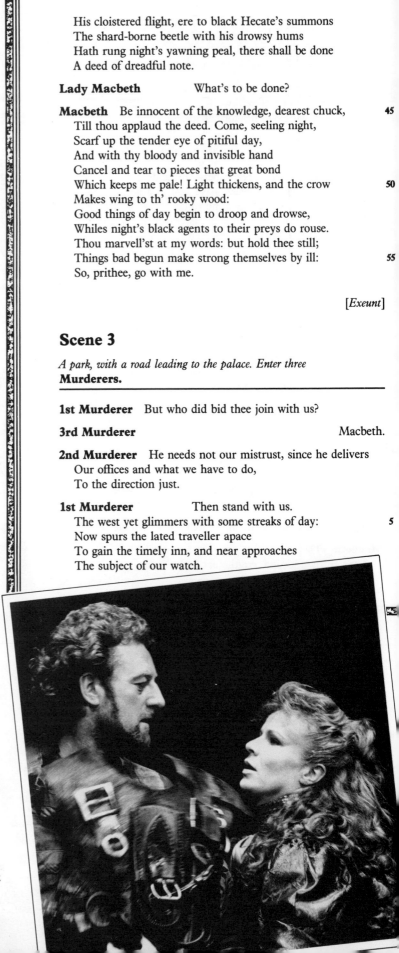

Be innocent of the knowledge, dearest chuck

Leicester Haymarket 1985

3rd Murderer   Hark! I hear horses.

Banquo   Give us a light there, ho!

2nd Murderer   Then 'tis he; the rest
That are within the note of expectation   10
Already are i'th' court.

1st Murderer   His horses go about.

3rd Murderer   Almost a mile: but he does usually –
So all men do – from thence to th' palace gate
Make it their walk.

[*Enter* **Banquo** *and* **Fleance** *with a torch*]

2nd Murderer   A light, a light!

3rd Murderer   'Tis he.

1st Murderer   Stand to't.   15

Banquo   It will be rain tonight.

1st Murderer   Let it come down.

[*They set upon* **Banquo**]

Banquo   O, treachery! Fly, good Fleance, fly, fly, fly!
Thou mayst revenge. O slave!

[*He dies.* **Fleance** *escapes*]

3rd Murderer   Who did strike out the light?

1st Murderer   Was't not the way?

3rd Murderer   There's but one down; the son is fled.

2nd Murderer   We have lost
Best half of our affair.   20

1st Murderer   Well, let's away, and say how much is done.

[*Exeunt*]

10   **within . . . expectation**   on the list of expected
guests
11   **go about**   are taking the long route round (to the
stables)
15   **Stand to't**   get ready
16   **Let it come down**   To what is the 1st Murderer
referring?
SD   **Fleance escapes**   In what way could this be
called the turning point in the play?
18   **way**   thing to do
20   **Best half of our affair**   the most important part of
our business

'A good man unjustly murdered.'
'One who becomes as corrupt as Macbeth
and therefore deserves his fate.'
What is your opinion of Banquo?

RSC 1976

1 **degrees** seating according to rank
1–2 **at first/And last** The meaning of this is unclear. Either (i) once and for all, or (ii) from the beginning to the end of the feast, or (iii) to all, whatever your rank. Which reading do you prefer?
4 **society** the present company
6–7 Our hostess is remaining seated on her throne, but at the most suitable time we shall request her to welcome you all.
SD When does Macbeth notice the murderer? How would you stage this?
10 **encounter** answer
How, perhaps, should the lords show their thanks?
11 **sides** that is, of the table
12 **large** unrestrained
15 His blood is better on the outside of you than inside him.
20 **the non-pareil** without equal

Scene 4

The hall of the palace. A banquet prepared. Enter **Macbeth, Lady Macbeth, Ross, Lennox, Lords** *and* **Attendants.**

Macbeth   You know your own degrees, sit down: at first
And last the hearty welcome.

Lords   Thanks to your majesty.

Macbeth   Ourself will mingle with society,
And play the humble host: 5
Our hostess keeps her state, but in best time
We will require her welcome.

Lady Macbeth   Pronounce it for me, sir, to all our friends,
For my heart speaks they are welcome.

[*Enter* **First Murderer** *at the door*]

Macbeth   See, they encounter thee with the hearts'   10
thanks.
Both sides are even: here I'll sit i'th' midst:
Be large in mirth, anon we'll drink a measure
The table round.
[*To* **Murderer**] There's blood upon thy face.

1st Murderer   'Tis Banquo's then.

Macbeth   'Tis better thee without than he within.   15
Is he dispatched?

1st Murderer   My lord, his throat is cut; that I did for him.

Macbeth   Thou art the best o'th cut-throats. Yet he's good
That did the like for Fleance: if thou didst it,
Thou art the nonpareil.   20

1st Murderer   Most royal sir – Fleance is 'scaped.

**at first
And last the hearty welcome**
Great Eastern Stage 1985

Macbeth   Then comes my fit again: I had else been perfect;
Whole as the marble, founded as the rock,
As broad and general as the casing air:
But now I am cabin'd, cribb'd, confin'd, bound in   25
To saucy doubts and fears. But Banquo's safe?

1st Murderer   Ay, my good lord: safe in a ditch he bides,
With twenty trenchèd gashes on his head;
The least a death to nature.

Macbeth   Thanks for that:
There the grown serpent lies; the worm that's fled   30
Hath nature that in time will venom breed,
No teeth for th' present. Get thee gone; to-morrow
We'll hear ourselves again.

                              [*Exit* **Murderer**]

Lady Macbeth   My royal lord,
You do not give the cheer. The feast is sold
That is not often vouched, while 'tis a-making,   35
'Tis given with welcome: to feed were best at home;
From thence the sauce to meat is ceremony;
Meeting were bare without it.

[*The ghost of* **Banquo** *enters and sits in Macbeth's place.*]

Macbeth   Sweet remembrancer!
Now good digestion wait on appetite,
And health on both!

Lennox   May't please your highness sit?   40

Macbeth   Here had we now our country's honour roofed,
Were the graced person of our Banquo present;
Who may I rather challenge for unkindness
Than pity for mischance!

Ross   His absence, sir,
Lays blame upon his promise. Please't your highness   45
To grace us with your royal company?

22   see Act III Scene 1 lines 106–7
23   **Whole**   solid
      founded   firm
24   as free as the surrounding air
25   **cabin'd, cribb'd, confin'd**   all mean 'shut up in a
      small space'
      What is the effect of the alliteration?
26   **saucy**   insolent
28   **trenchèd**   (pronounced as two syllables): cut deep
      as a trench
29   **nature**   any living thing
30–2 see Act III scene 2 lines 13–15, and the illustration
      of the Banquo family tree
30   **worm**   young snake
33   **hear ourselves**   discuss it
34–7 You are not (i) encouraging conviviality; (ii) leading
      the toasting. A feast is like a meal which is paid for
      if it is not frequently sprinkled with words of
      welcome during the eating of it: mere satisfying of
      hunger is best done at home; when away from
      home, courtesy adds spice to the meal.
38   **Meeting**   (i) meeting in company; (ii) eating
      meat
      This is the kind of pun that Shakespeare loves to
      use in any context, comic or tragic.
39   **wait on**   attend
41   **honour roofed**   nobility under one roof
42   **graced**   gracious
43   **challenge for unkindness**   accuse of bad
      manners
44   **pity for mischance**   worry that some accident
      has happened to him (what hypocritical irony!)
44–5 **His absence . . . promise**   He should not have
      promised to be here, sir, if he could not manage it.

Then comes my fit again
Great Eastern Stage 1985

49 moves disturbs
50 Nowadays it is fashionable for no ghost to appear, emphasising that it is in Macbeth's imagination; whereas Shakespeare instructs that a ghost appears to Macbeth and the audience (although, of course, nobody else on stage sees it). How would you direct this episode?
56 upon a thought in a moment, as quickly as thought
57 much you note take much notice of
58 extend his passion prolong his fit
61 proper stuff fine behaviour (sarcastic)
62 painting that is, not a real thing
63 air-drawn (i) drawn in the air; (ii) drawn through the air
64 flaws gusts, outbursts
65 to compared to
67 Authoriz'd by her grandam approved of by her grandmother; in other words, a harmless old wives' tale
72 charnel-houses vaults in which were stored the bones of long-buried bodies which had been dug up

Prithee, see there! behold! look! lo! how say you?

Northcott Theatre 1986

Macbeth	The table's full.
Lennox	Here is a place reserved, sir.
Macbeth	Where?
Lennox	Here, my good lord. What is't that moves your highness?
Macbeth	Which of you have done this? 50
Lords	What, my good lord?

Macbeth   Thou canst not say I did it: never shake
Thy gory locks at me.

Ross   Gentlemen, rise, his highness is not well.

Lady Macbeth   Sit, worthy friends: my lord is often thus,
And hath been from his youth: pray you, keep seat,   55
The fit is momentary; upon a thought
He will again be well: if much you note him,
You shall offend him and extend his passion:
Feed, and regard him not.
[*To* **Macbeth,** *aside*]   Are you a man?

Macbeth   Ay, and a bold one, that dare look on that   60
Which might appal the devil.

Lady Macbeth   O proper stuff!
This is the very painting of your fear:
This is the air-drawn dagger which, you said,
Led you to Duncan. O, these flaws and starts,
Impostors to true fear, would well become   65
A woman's story at a winter's fire,
Authoriz'd by her grandam. Shame itself!
Why do you make such faces? When all's done,
You look but on a stool.

Macbeth   Prithee, see there! behold! look! lo! how say you?   70
Why, what care I? If thou canst nod, speak too.
If charnel-houses and our graves must send

Those that we bury back, our monuments
Shall be the maws of kites.

[*The **Ghost** vanishes*]

Lady Macbeth   What! quite unmanned in folly?

Macbeth   If I stand here, I saw him.

Lady Macbeth   Fie, for shame!   75

Macbeth   Blood hath been shed ere now, i'th'olden time,
Ere humane statute purged the gentle weal;
Ay, and since too, murders have been performed
Too terrible for the ear: the time has been,
That, when the brains were out, the man would die,   80
And there an end: but now they rise again,
With twenty mortal murders on their crowns,
And push us from our stools. This is more strange
Than such a murder is.

Lady Macbeth   My worthy lord,
Your noble friends do lack you.

Macbeth   I do forget.   85
Do not muse at me, my most worthy friends;
I have a strange infirmity, which is nothing
To those that know me. Come, love and health to all;
Then I'll sit down. Give me some wine, fill full.

[*The **Ghost** returns*]

I drink to th' general joy o'th' whole table,   90
And to our dear friend Banquo, whom we miss;
Would he were here! to all, and him we thirst,
And all to all!

Lords   Our duties, and the pledge.

Macbeth   Avaunt! and quit my sight! let the earth hide thee!
Thy bones are marrowless, thy blood is cold;   95

73–4 **monuments . . . kites** We shall have to give their remains as food to carrion birds.
77 **statute . . . weal** laws cleansed society and made it civilised
82 **mortal . . . crowns** fatal wounds on their heads
89 **Then** that is, after my toast
92 **thirst** desire to drink
93 **all to all** either (i) all good wishes to all, or (ii) let everybody toast everybody else
Our . . . pledge We offer our homage and drink the toast.
94 **Avaunt!** Away!

What evidence is there on this page that a part of Macbeth respects – even loves – the human law which he flouts?

Fie, for shame!

Northcott Theatre 1986

96 **speculation** comprehension
98 **of custom** which regularly occurs
102 **Hyrcan** from Hyrcania, near the Caspian Sea
103 **that** that is, a ghost
105 **to the desert** to fight in a lonely place
106 **inhabit** have in me
    protest declare
107 **baby** doll
111 **admired** wondered at, astounding
112 **overcome** pass over
113– **strange ... owe** wonder about my own
14 character/mind
115 **you** that is, the assembled company
117 **mine is blanched** my cheeks are made white
119 **at once, goodnight** I say goodnight to all of you
    at once (and not individually as you leave, as one
    might expect a hostess to do)
120 Do not bother about leaving in proper order
    according to your rank.

How do you think Lady Macbeth is feeling at
this point in the play about her position, her
husband, her relationship with him, and
herself? You could write in the form of an
entry in Lady Macbeth's diary.

As a director, what would you want to
communicate to an audience about Banquo's
ghost, and how would you do it?

Draw diagrams showing how you would
arrange the set for this scene.

Compile a props list for this scene.

Line 101: The bear-baiting pit was only a street away
from the Globe Theatre, and the audiences would
doubtless have been able to hear the bears growling in
their cages.

Thou hast no speculation in those eyes
Which thou dost glare with!

Lady Macbeth   Think of this, good peers,
But as a thing of custom: 'tis no other;
Only it spoils the pleasure of the time.

Macbeth   What man dare, I dare: 100
Approach thou like the rugged Russian bear,
The armed rhinoceros, or th'Hyrcan tiger,
Take any shape but that, and my firm nerves
Shall never tremble: or be alive again,
And dare me to the desert with thy sword;   105
If trembling I inhabit then, protest me
The baby of a girl. Hence, horrible shadow!
Unreal mock'ry, hence!

[*The* **Ghost** *goes*]

                              Why, so; being gone'
I am a man again. Pray you, sit still.

Lady Macbeth   You have displaced the mirth, broke
    the good meeting,   110
With most admired disorder.

Macbeth   Can such things be,
And overcome us like a summer's cloud,
Without our special wonder? You make me strange
Even to the disposition that I owe,
When now I think you can behold such sights,   115
And keep the natural ruby of your cheeks,
When mine is blanched with fear.

Ross   What sights, my lord?

Lady Macbeth   I pray you, speak not; he grows worse
    and worse;
Question enrages him: at once, good night.
Stand not upon the order of your going,   120
But go at once.

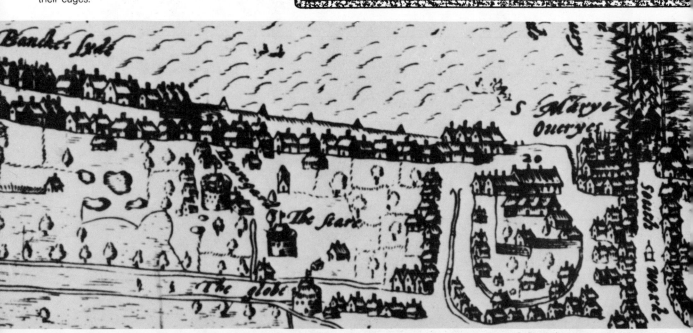

Lennox   Good night, and better health
Attend his majesty!

Lady Macbeth   A kind good night to all!

[They leave]

Macbeth   It will have blood; they say, blood will have blood:
Stones have been known to move and trees to speak;
Augurs and understood relations have   125
By magot-pies and choughs and rooks brought forth
The secret'st man of blood. What is the night?

Lady Macbeth   Almost at odds with morning, which is which.

Macbeth   How say'st thou, that Macduff denies his person
At our great bidding?

Lady Macbeth   Did you send to him, sir?   130

Macbeath   I hear it by the way; but I will send:
There's not a one of them but in his house
I keep a servant fee'd. I will to-morrow,
And betimes I will, to the Weird Sisters:
More shall they speak; for now I am bent to know,   135
By the worst means, the worst. For mine own good
All causes shall give way: I am in blood
Stepped in so far that, should I wade no more,
Returning were as tedious as go o'er:
Strange things I have in head that will to hand,   140
Which must be acted ere they may be scanned.

Lady Macbeth   You lack the season of all natures, sleep.

Macbeth   Come, we'll to sleep. My strange and self-abuse
Is the initiate fear that wants hard use:
We are yet but young in deed.   145

[Exeunt]

123   **It** (i) the murder of Banquo; (ii) Banquo's ghost
124   He means that such supernatural happenings have disclosed murders (perhaps stones covering a dead body fell away; voices coming from trees was a common superstition).
125   **Augurs** prophecies
        understood relations the connection between events
126   **magot-pies** magpies
        choughs any kind of 'chattering' bird such as crows or jackdaws
127   **man of blood** murderer
        night time of night
128   **at odds** conflicting
        It may be significant that, as the play passes its midpoint, there is the hope of a new dawn for Scotland. How may lines 129–30 be seen as reinforcing this idea?
129   what do you say to the fact that Macduff refuses to come . . . ?
132   **them** that is, the lords whom Macbeth suspects
133   **fee'd** bribed to spy and inform
134   **betimes** early
135   **bent** determined
137   **causes** (other) considerations
        give way take second place
140   **Strange** Again, this word carries a sense of 'unnatural'.
        will to hand must be put into action
141   **may be scanned** can be thought about
142   **season** preservative (as in food)
143   **strange and self-abuse** unnatural delusions
144   **initiate fear** the fear of a novice
        wants hard use lacks the practice which hardens one
145   **We** Is he using the royal 'we', meaning himself alone, or is he including his wife in his thoughts of further crimes?

With close reference to the text, discuss (a) Lady Macbeth's great resourcefulness in covering up for her husband during this episode, and (b) the signs that she is emotionally exhausted after the nobles leave.

This is the last time we see a sane Lady Macbeth in the play. Look back at her character as it has revealed itself since we first saw her reading from Macbeth's letter in Act I Scene 5.

Assess the importance of this scene in the play.

It will have blood
Leicester Haymarket 1985

2 beldams hags
7 close secret
15 pit of Acheron a cave in hell
21 Unto a dismal preparing for a disastrous
22 wrought done
23–9 There was a belief that the moon shed an enchanted liquid on certain plants and places.
24 profound (i) heavy; (ii) having deep magical properties
26 sleights arts
27 artificial sprites spirits raised by magic art (see the apparitions of Act IV Scene 1)
29 confusion ruin, destruction
30 spurn ignore
30–1 bear . . . fear Hecate says that the witches' illusions will give him a wild hope that will overcome his commonsense, moral sense, and natural sense of fear.
32 security over-confidence, a false sense of security

Scene 5

A heath. Enter the three **Witches***, meeting* **Hecate***.*

1st Witch   Why, how now, Hecate, you look angerly.

Hecate   Have I not reason, beldams as you are,
   Saucy and overbold? How did you dare
   To trade and traffic with Macbeth
   In riddles and affairs of death;   5
   And I, the mistress of your charms,
   The close contriver of all harms,
   Was never called to bear my part,
   Or show the glory of our art?
   And, which is worse, all you have done   10
   Hath been but for a wayward son,
   Spiteful and wrathful, who (as others do)
   Loves for his own ends, not for you.
   But make amends now: get you gone,
   And at the pit of Acheron   15
   Meet me i'th' morning: thither he
   Will come to know his destiny.
   Your vessels and your spells provide,
   Your charms and everything beside.
   I am for th'air; this night I'll spend   20
   Unto a dismal and a fatal end.
   Great business must be wrought ere noon:
   Upon the corner of the moon
   There hangs a vap'rous drop profound:
   I'll catch it ere it come to ground: 25
   And that distilled by magic sleights
   Shall raise such artificial sprites
   As by the strength of their illusion
   Shall draw him on to his confusion.
   He shall spurn fate, scorn death, and bear   30
   His hopes 'bove wisdom, grace, and fear:
   And you all know security
   Is mortals' chiefest enemy.

Many consider that this scene was not written by Shakespeare, and it is often cut in modern productions.

In what way do you think that the scene may be seen as not fitting into the play?

How does the rhythm of Hecate's verse differ from that elsewhere in the play?

[*Music and a song: 'Come away, come away*
Hecate, Hecate, come away!']

Hark, I am called: my little spirit, see,
Sits in a foggy cloud, and stays for me.   35

[*She flies away*]

1st Witch   Come, let's make haste; she'll soon be back again.

[*They vanish*]

Scene 6

Somewhere near Forres. Enter **Lennox** *and another* **Lord**.

Lennox   My former speeches have but hit your thoughts,
Which can interpret farther: only I say
Things have been strangely borne. The gracious Duncan
Was pitied of Macbeth: marry, he was dead:
And the right valiant Banquo walked too late –   5
Whom you may say, if 't please you, Fleance killed,
For Fleance fled: men must not walk too late.
Who cannot want the thought, how monstrous
It was for Malcolm and for Donalbain
To kill their gracious father? damned fact!   10
How it did grieve Macbeth! did he not straight,
In pious rage, the two delinquents tear,
That were the slaves of drink and thralls of sleep?
Was not that nobly done? Ay, and wisely too;
For 'twould have angered any heart alive   15
To hear the men deny't. So that, I say,
He has borne all things well: and I do think
That, had he Duncan's sons under his key –
As, an't please heaven, he shall not – they should find
What 'twere to kill a father; so should Fleance.   20
But, peace! for from broad words, and 'cause he failed
His presence at the tyrant's feast, I hear,

34 little attendant, familiar (see Act I Scene 1)

1 My former speeches Since the banquet the nobility have been discussing recent events. The opening of this scene gives a sense of a continuation of what is happening off-stage. Can you find any other scene opening where this occurs?
but hit only coincided with
2 Which . . . farther from which you can draw your own conclusions
3 borne managed, carried out
4 of by
8 want the thought help thinking
10 fact evil deed
11 straight straightaway
12 pious loyal
13 thralls slaves (that is, the two grooms)
15 'twould it would
16 deny't that is, deny that they had murdered the king
17 well successfully and cunningly
19 an't if it
21 from broad words because of frankly speaking his mind
What has Macduff been saying? And upon what occasion? Write a short scene in which Macduff speaks his mind.
'cause because

What do you think is an appropriate tone of voice with which Lennox delivers this speech? Practise delivering it, using a tape recorder to help you; and then make a recording of yourself as Lennox.

25 holds the due of birth withholds his birthright (that is, the throne of Scotland)
27 Of by
Edward Edward the Confessor
Find out when he reigned, and what his reputation was. This will help you to see how Shakespeare is contrasting England under Edward and Scotland under Macbeth.
28-9 nothing ... respect in no way lessens the high respect in which he (Macduff) is held
30 upon his aid in support of him (Malcolm)
31 wake rouse into action
Northumberland either (i) the Earl of Northumberland, or (ii) the people of Northumberland whose territory borders on Scotland
35 Free remove
bloody knives the knives of murderers
36 free freely granted
38 exasperate exasperated
40 absolute curt, dismissive
41 cloudy scowling, surly
me used for emphasis
42 who should if he would
43 clogs burdens
The messenger is aware that Macbeth may treat badly one who brings bad news (see Act V Scene 3 and Act V Scene 5).
that the messenger's behaviour
44 him to a caution Macduff to be careful
hold keep

What information do we learn in this scene? Why do you think it is put into the mouths of minor characters?

How does the scene create a sense of growing fear in Scotland? What signs of hope are there?

It is clear that Lennox has been doing some hard thinking since we last saw him. Write a letter which at this point he might have written and sent to Macduff in England.

Macduff lives in disgrace. Sir, can you tell
Where he bestows himself?

Lord   The son of Duncan,
From whom this tyrant holds the due of birth,   25
Lives in the English court, and is received
Of the most pious Edward with such grace
That the malevolence of fortune nothing
Takes from his high respect. Thither Macduff
Is gone to pray the holy king, upon his aid   30
To wake Northumberland and warlike Siward,
That by the help of these – with Him above
To ratify the work – we may again
Give to our tables meat, sleep to our nights;
Free from our feasts and banquets bloody knives;   35
Do faithful homage and receive free honours;
All which we pine for now. And this report
Hath so exasperate the king that he
Prepares for some attempt of war.

Lennox   Sent he to Macduff?

Lord   He did: and with an absolute 'Sir, not I',   40
The cloudy messenger turns me his back,
And hums, as who should say, 'You'll rue the time
That clogs me with this answer.'

Lennox   And that well might
Advise him to a caution, to hold what distance
His wisdom can provide. Some holy angel   45
Fly to the court of England and unfold
His message ere he come, that a swift blessing
May soon return to this our suffering country
Under a hand accursed!

Lord   I'll send my prayers with him.

                                                    [*Exeunt*]

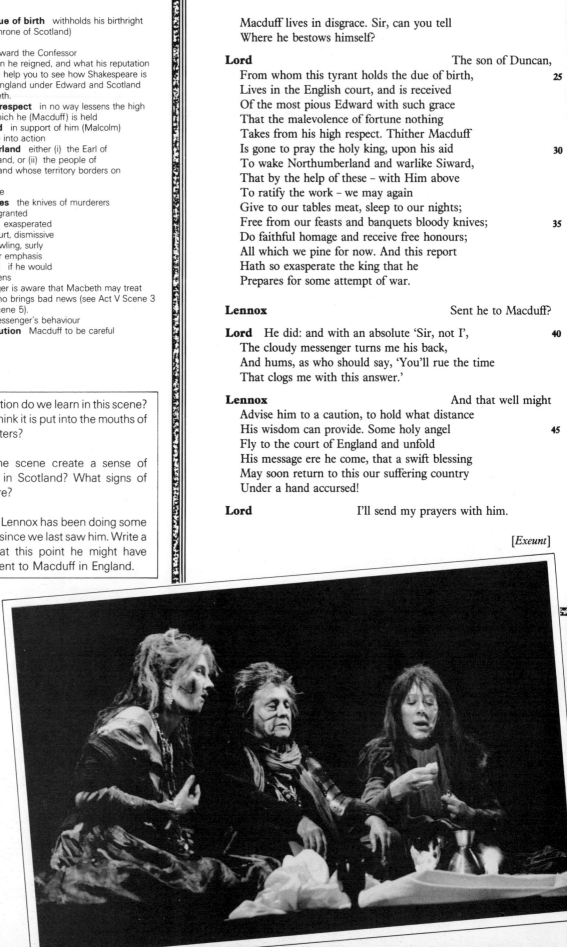

RSC 1986

Act IV

Scene 1

A dark cavern. In the middle a fiery cauldron. Thunder.
Enter the three **Witches.**

1st Witch   Thrice the brinded cat hath mewed.

2nd Witch   Thrice, and once the hedge-pig whined.

3rd Witch   Harpier cries: 'Tis time, 'tis time.

1st Witch   Round about the cauldron go:
In the poisoned entrails throw.   5
Toad, that under cold stone
Days and nights has thirty-one
Sweltered venom sleeping got,
Boil thou first i'th' charmed pot!

All   Double, double toil and trouble;   10
Fire, burn; and cauldron, bubble.

2nd Witch   Fillet of a fenny snake,
In the cauldron boil and bake:
Eye of newt and toe of frog,
Wool of bat and tongue of dog,   15
Adder's fork and blind-worm's sting,
Lizard's leg and howlet's wing,
For a charm of powerful trouble,
Like a hell-broth boil and bubble.

All   Double, double toil and trouble: 20
Fire, burn; and cauldron, bubble.

3rd Witch   Scale of dragon, tooth of wolf,
Witch's mummy, maw and gulf
Of the ravined salt-sea shark,
Root of hemlock digged i'th' dark,   25
Liver of blaspheming Jew,

1 **brinded** streaky coloured
2 **hedge-pig** hedgehog
3 **Harpier** the 3rd Witch's familiar spirit
   'Tis time presumably, time to begin the spell
8 The toad has sweated out poison whilst sleeping.
12 slice of a marsh-snake
16 **fork** forked tongue
17 **howlet's** owl's
23 witches' dried flesh, stomach and gullet
24 **ravined** gorged with the flesh of its victim(s) (see Act II Scene 4 line 28)
25 Digging up poisonous hemlock at night was supposed to increase its powers.

Look at the rhythm of the witches' speech. What is the dramatic effect of giving them lines which have one beat less than the blank verse in which most of the play is written?

Round about the cauldron go
Torch Theatre 1986

26–30　**Jew...Turk...Tartar...birth-strangled babe** (and therefore not baptised) are all non-Christian
27　**slips**　shavings (yew was considered to be poisonous)
31　born to a prostitute in a ditch
32　**slab**　sticky
33　**chaudron**　entrails
SD　The appearance of Hecate and her lines are
39–43　probably not by Shakespeare, and are usually cut in performance.
39　**pains**　trouble
44　Sudden unaccountable pains in the body were supposed to give warning of coming events.
48　**black**　because they practise black magic
50　**conjure**　call upon
　　that　that is, black magic
　　profess　practise
51　Macbeth does not care how evil they are (even if their knowledge comes from the devil).
52　**untie**　let loose

Compose a recipe, fair or foul, in the style and rhythm of the witches.

Gall of goat and slips of yew
Slivered in the moon's eclipse,
Nose of Turk and Tartar's lips,
Finger of birth-strangled babe　　　　　　30
Ditch-delivered by a drab,
Make the gruel thick and slab:
Add thereto a tiger's chaudron,
For th'ingredience of our cauldron.

All　Double, double toil and trouble;　　35
Fire, burn; and cauldron, bubble.

2nd Witch　Cool it with a baboon's blood,
Then the charm is firm and good.

[*Enter* **Hecate**]

Hecate　O, well done! I commend your pains,
And every one shall share i'th' gains:　　40
And now about the cauldron sing,
Like elves and fairies in a ring,
Enchanting all that you put in.

[*Music and a song: Black spirits.* **Hecate** *goes*]

2nd Witch　By the pricking of my thumbs,
Something wicked this way comes:
Open, locks,　　　　　　　　　　　　45
Whoever knocks!

[*Enter* **Macbeth**]

Macbeth　How now, you secret, black, and midnight hags!
What is't you do?

All　　　　　　　　　A deed without a name.

Macbeth　I conjure you, by that which you profess　　50
Howe'er you come to know it, answer me:
Though you untie the winds and let them fight

**By the pricking of my thumbs,
Something wicked this way comes**

Leicester Haymarket 1985

Against the churches; though the yesty waves
Confound and swallow navigation up;
Though bladed corn be lodged and trees blown down;   55
Though castles topple on their warders' heads;
Though palaces and pyramids do slope
Their heads to their foundations; though the treasure
Of Nature's germens tumble all together,
Even till destruction sicken; answer me   60
To what I ask you.

1st Witch   Speak.

2nd Witch   Demand.

3rd Witch   We'll answer.

1st Witch   Say if th'hadst rather hear it from our mouths,
Or from our masters.

Macbeth   Call 'em, let me see 'em!

1st Witch   Pour in sow's blood, that hath eaten
Her nine farrow; grease that's sweaten   65
From the murderer's gibbet throw
Into the flame.

All   Come, high or low;
Thyself and office deftly show.

[*Thunder.* **First Apparition:** *an armed head*]

Macbeth   Tell me, thou unknown power –

1st Witch   He knows thy thought:
Hear his speech, but say thou nought.   70

1st Apparition   Macbeth! Macbeth! Macbeth! beware
      Macduff,
Beware the thane of Fife. Dismiss me. Enough.

[*Descends*]

53 **yesty** foaming
55 **bladed** unripe
      lodged beaten down
57 **pyramids do slope** towers bend
59 **Nature's germens** the very seeds of life
60 **sicken** is sick and tired at its own work
50–61 What does this speech tell you about Macbeth's
      reckless state of mind?
65 **farrow** litter
68 **office** your works
71–2 To what event does the 'armed head' look forward?

Speak.

Demand.

We'll answer.

RSC 1976

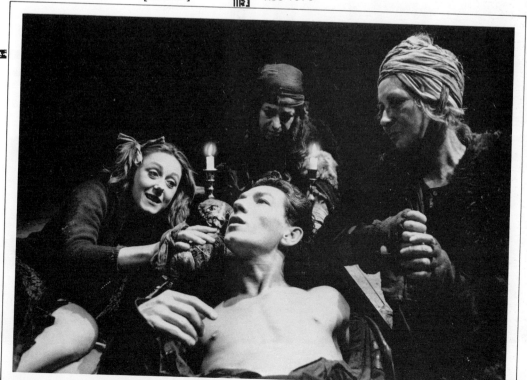

74 harped touched upon, guessed
SD Who do you think is the 'bloody child'?
84 take ... fate guarantee fate's promise
SD Who and what does the Third Apparition signify?
87 issue child
88-9 round/And top crown
This also suggests the summit of Macbeth's
ambition (see Act I Scene 5 line 27).
93 Birnam wood and Dunsinane are about 12 miles
apart.

Macbeth Whate'er thou art, for thy good caution thanks;
Thou hast harped my fear aright. But one word more –

1st Witch He will not be commanded: here's another,   75
More potent than the first.

[*Thunder.* **Second Apparition:** *a bloody child*]

2nd Apparition Macbeth! Macbeth! Macbeth!

Macbeth Had I three ears, I'd hear thee.

2nd Apparition Be bloody, bold, and resolute: laugh to scorn
The power of man; for none of woman born   80
Shall harm Macbeth.

[*Descends*]

Macbeth Then live, Macduff: what need I fear of thee?
But yet I'll make assurance double sure,
And take a bond of fate: thou shalt not live,
That I may tell pale-hearted fear it lies,   85
And sleep in spite of thunder.

[*Thunder.* **Third Apparition:** *a child crowned, with a tree in his hand*]

What is this,
That rises like the issue of a king,
And wears upon his baby-brow the round
And top of sovereignty?

All Listen, but speak not to't.

3rd Apparition Be lion-mettled, proud, and take no care   90
Who chafes, who frets, or where conspirers are:
Macbeth shall never vanquished be until
Great Birnam wood to high Dunsinane hill
Shall come against him.

[*Descends*]

What is this
That rises like the issue of a king
Engraving from Bell's edition of *Shakespeare*, 1773

Royal Lyceum 1986

Macbeth   That will never be;
Who can impress the forest, bid the tree   95
Unfix his earth-bound root? Sweet bodements! good!
Rebellious dead, rise never, till the wood
Of Birnam rise, and our high-placed Macbeth
Shall live the lease of nature, pay his breath
To time and mortal custom. Yet my heart   100
Throbs to know one thing; tell me, if your art
Can tell so much: shall Banquo's issue ever
Reign in this kingdom?

All   Seek to know no more.

Macbeth   I will be satisfied: deny me this,
And an eternal curse fall on you! Let me know. –   105
Why sinks that cauldron? and what noise is this?

                              [*Oboes play*]

1st Witch   Show!

2nd Witch   Show

3rd Witch   Show!

All   Show his eyes, and grieve his heart;   110
Come like shadows, so depart.

[*A show of eight* **Kings,** *the last with a glass in his hand;*
Banquo's Ghost *following.*]

Macbeth   Thou art too like the spirit of Banquo: down!
Thy crown does sear mine eye-balls. And thy hair,
Thou other gold-bound brow, is like the first.
A third is like the former. Filthy hags!   115
Why do you show me this? – A fourth? Start, eyes!
What, will the line stretch out to th' crack of doom?
Another yet? A seventh? I'll see no more:
And yet the eighth appears, who bears a glass
Which shows me many more; and some I see   120

94–   What is the dramatic effect of making Macbeth
101   continue in rhyming couplets?
95   **impress**   conscript
96   **bodements**   omens, prophecies
99   **lease of nature**   natural lifespan (see Act III Scene
2 line 38)
99–   **pay ... custom**   die a natural death
100
106   **noise**   the oboes
What mood do they create at this moment (see Act
I Scene 6)?
111   **shadows**   a name sometimes used to mean 'actor'
or 'player'
Shakespeare often used imagery drawn directly
from the theatre.
SD   **show**   a dumb show or mime of the kind which
was common on the Elizabethan stage
113   **sear**   burn
116   **Start**   that is, from your sockets
117   **crack of doom**   thunder at the Judgment Day
119   **eighth**   James VI of Scotland and I of England
Macbeth has been shown the Stuart line leading up
to James, and then in a magic mirror ('glass') held
by James sees more descendants.
Shakespeare is flattering his monarch and
suggesting that his posterity is secure. In the light of
history, can you detect a nice irony here?

Contrast Macbeth's interpretation of the
three apparitions with what they actually
signified.

Macbeth and the witches. Engraving by Guernier
from Pope's *Works of Shakespeare*, 1728

121 This refers to the combined coronation regalia ('balls' = orbs) of Scotland and England, united as one kingdom by James's accession to the English throne in 1603.
123 **boltered** matted, plastered
130 **antic round** Ben Jonson, a playwright who was a contemporary of Shakespeare, describes a fantastic and grotesque round dance as follows: 'a *magical Daunce* full of praeposterous change and gesticulation . . . dauncing, back to back, hip to hip, theyr handes joyn'd, and making theyr *circles* backward to the left hand, with strange, phantastique motions of theyr heads and bodyes'.
131-2 Is this a reference to Macbeth? Or to James I, who may have been sitting in the audience at a special performance? Or to both?
134 **aye** ever
135 **without there** you who wait outside
139 How ironic! And how little Macbeth now seems to be aware of himself.

'The witches cannot be held responsible for any of Macbeth's actions.' Discuss.

How has Macbeth been affected by his visit to the witches? Look closely at how he behaves in Act V.

Why does Lennox still serve Macbeth, despite the tone of his remarks in Act III Scene 6? Write an entry in Lennox's diary which may have been written since his last appearance.

That two-fold balls and treble sceptres carry.
Horrible sight! Now I see 'tis true,
For the blood-boltered Banquo smiles upon me,
And points at them for his. What, is this so?

1st Witch   Ay, sir, all this is so. But why   125
Stands Macbeth thus amazedly?
Come, sisters, cheer we up his sprites,
And show the best of our delights.
I'll charm the air to give a sound,
While you perform your antic round: 130
That this great king may kindly say
Our duties did his welcome pay.

[*Music. The* **Witches** *dance, and vanish.*]

Macbeth   Where are they? Gone? Let this pernicious hour
Stand aye accursed in the calendar
Come in, without there!   135

[*Enter* **Lennox**]

Lennox   What's your grace's will?

Macbeth   Saw you the Weird Sisters?

Lennox   No, my lord.

Macbeth   Came they not by you?

Lennox   No indeed, my lord.

Macbeth   Infected by the air whereon they ride,
And damned all those that trust them! I did hear
The galloping of horse. Who was't came by?   140

Lennox   'Tis two or three, my lord, that bring you word
Macduff is fled to England.

Macbeth   Fled to England!

Lennox   Ay, my good lord.

Crucible Theatre 1985

Macbeth   Time, thou anticipat'st my dread exploits:
The flighty purpose never is o'ertook   145
Unless the deed go with it. From this moment
The very firstlings of my heart shall be
The firstlings of my hand. And even now
To crown my thoughts with acts, be it thought and done:
The castle of Macduff I will surprise,   150
Seize upon Fife, give to th'edge o'th'sword
His wife, his babes, and all unfortunate souls
That trace him in his line. No boasting like a fool;
This deed I'll do before this purpose cool.
But no more sights! Where are these gentlemen?   155
Come, bring me where they are.

[Exeunt]

Scene 2

Fife, Macduff's castle. Enter **Lady Macduff,** *her* **Son,**
and **Ross.**

Lady Macduff   What has he done, to make him fly the land?

Ross   You must have patience, madam.

Lady Macduff   He had none:
His flight was madness: when our actions do not,
Our fears do make us traitors.

Ross   You know not
Whether it was his wisdom or his fear.   5

Lady Macduff   Wisdom! to leave his wife, to leave his babes,
His mansion and his titles, in a place
From whence himself does fly? He loves us not;
He wants the natural touch: for the poor wren,
The most diminutive of birds, will fight,   10
Her young ones in her nest, against the owl.
All is the fear and nothing is the love;
As little is the wisdom, where the flight
So runs against all reason.

144   **anticipat'st**   forestall
What 'dread exploits' do you think Macbeth was planning?
145–6   **flighty . . . with it**   Macbeth is saying that plans do not get carried out unless put quickly into action.
147   **firstlings**   first impulses
Macbeth is allowing emotion to replace reason, a failing which Shakespeare shows in other plays (e.g. Antony in *Antony and Cleopatra*). Macbeth quickly decides on a pointless revenge against Macduff. In what ways will these murders differ from Macbeth's former crimes?
153   **trace . . . line**   follow him
155   **sights**   apparitions

Write out Macbeth's final speech in Scene 1 and then scan it, putting accent marks over the syllables which you think should be stressed.

1   **he**   Macduff
How does Shakespeare here give us the feeling that the conversation is a continuation of one that has been going on off-stage?
3–4   **His flight . . . traitors**   In the light of these words, examine the part played by Macduff after the accession of Macbeth.
4   **makes us**   makes us look like
6–8   Why do you think Macduff fled without informing his wife?
7   **titles**   all those things to which a person is entitled; that is, possessions
9   **wants the natural touch**   lacks natural feelings of affection and protectiveness
Do you think that Lady Macduff really believes what she says here?
12   all he thinks of is fear for himself and not at all of love for us (see the Bible, 1 John 4:18)

Leicester Haymarket 1985

14 **coz** cousin
15 **school** control
    for as for
17 **fits o'th'season** troubles of the times
18 **are** are regarded as
19 **know** know it
19–20 **hold rumour/From** believe rumours inspired by
22 **Each ... move** Critics disagree as to the meaning of this: some think that Ross suddenly breaks off what he is saying; some that 'move' should read 'more' or 'none'. What do you think?
23 **Shall** it shall – a sign that Ross is in a hurry?
24–5 **Things ... before** Are these words significant at this point in the play? 'Translate' them into modern English.
29 Ross means that he would weep, thus shaming himself and embarrassing Lady Macduff.
32 **with** on
34–5 **net ... gin** various ways of trapping birds
36 Why is this line pathetic (in the true sense) in view of what is about to happen? ('Pathetic' = that which is worthy of pathos or pity.) Shakespeare is showing us a scene of domestic innocence in order to highlight the senseless nature of the coming murders.

How much does Ross know of Macbeth's intentions? Why is he at the Macduff's castle?

In Polanski's 1971 film, Ross lets the murderers into the castle. Is there any justification for this interpretation? Or is Ross merely a servant who is increasingly opposed to his master's behaviour? Where is he in the next scene?

Ross   My dearest coz,
I pray you school yourself. But, for your husband,   15
He is noble, wise, judicious, and best knows
The fits o'th'season. I dare not speak much further,
But cruel are the times, when we are traitors
And do not know ourselves; when we hold rumour
From what we fear, yet know not what we fear,   20
But float upon a wild and violent sea,
Each way and move. I take my leave of you:
Shall not be long but I'll be here again:
Things at the worst will cease, or else climb upward
To what they were before. My pretty cousin,   25
Blessing upon you!

Lady Macduff Fathered he is, and yet he's fatherless.

Ross I am so much a fool, should I stay longer
It would be my disgrace and your discomfort.
I take my leave at once.   30

                                             [*Exit*]

Lady Macduff   Sirrah, your father's dead,
And what will you do now? How will you live?

Son As birds do, mother.

Lady Macduff   What, with worms and flies?

Son With what I get, I mean, and so do they.

Lady Macduff Poor bird! thou'ldst never fear the net nor lime,
The pitfall nor the gin.   35

Son Why should I, mother? Poor birds they are not set for.
My father is not dead, for all your saying.

Lady Macduff Yes, he is dead: how wilt thou do for a father?

Son Nay, how will you do for a husband?

Lady Macduff Why, I can buy me twenty at any market.   40

**My dearest coz,
I pray you school yourself.**

Leicester Haymarket 1985

Son Then you'll buy 'em to sell again.

Lady Macduff Thou speak'st with all thy wit, and yet i'faith
With wit enough for thee.

Son Was my father a traitor, mother?

Lady Macduff Ay, that he was. **45**

Son What is a traitor?

Lady Macduff Why, one that swears and lies.

Son And be all traitors that do so?

Lady Macduff Every one that does so is a traitor, and must be
hanged.

Son And must they all be hanged that swear and lie? **50**

Lady Macduff Every one.

Son Who must hang them?

Lady Macduff Why, the honest men.

Son Then the liars and swearers are fools; for there are liars
and swearers enow to beat the honest men and hang up them. **55**

Lady Macduff Now God help thee, poor monkey! But how
wilt thou do for a father?

Son If he were dead, you'ld weep for him: if you would not, it
were a good sign that I should quickly have a new father.

Lady Macduff Poor prattler, how thou talk'st! **60**

[*Enter a* **Messenger**]

Messenger Bless you, fair dame! I am not to you known,
Though in your state of honour I am perfect.
I doubt some danger does approach you nearly.
If you will take a homely man's advice,
Be not found here; hence, with your little ones. **65**
To fright you thus, methinks I am too savage;

47 **swears and lies** takes an oath and breaks it
Perhaps she is thinking of marriage vows, in that
her husband is apparently failing to love and
cherish her.
55 **enow** enough
62 although I am well aware of your noble rank
He has burst in on her unannounced, and is partly
apologising. The pace of the scene changes at this
point. Why the change from prose to verse?
63 **doubt** suspect, fear
64 **homely** ordinary, humble

. . . beat the honest men and hang up them.
Oxford Playhouse 1982

What would you say is the tone of the
conversation between Lady Macduff and
her son?

Find two examples on these pages which
show that the son is perceptive and
precocious.

67 To do worse that is, not to warn you in plain
terms
    fell savage, evil
68 nigh near
71-3 In what way are Lady Macduff's words a comment
on the scale of values which Macbeth has
established in Scotland.
81 fry of treachery offspring of a traitor
'Egg' and 'fry' are metaphors taken from fish,
unhatched and very young, respectively.

To do worse to you were fell cruelty,
Which is too nigh your person. Heaven preserve you!
I dare abide no longer.

[*Exit*]

Lady Macduff   Whither should I fly?
I have done no harm. But I remember now   70
I am in this earthly world; where to do harm
Is often laudable, to do good sometime
Accounted dangerous folly: why then, alas,
Do I put up that womanly defence,
To say I have done no harm?

[*Enter* **Murderers**]

                                What are these faces?   75

Murderer Where is your husband?

Lady Macduff I hope, in no place so unsanctified
Where such as thou mayst find him.

Murderer   He's a traitor.

Son Thou liest, thou shag-haired villain.

Murderer   What, you egg!   80
Young fry of treachery! [*Stabs him*]

Son   He has killed me, mother:
Run away, I pray you. [*Dies*]
[*Exit* **Lady Macduff** *crying 'Murder', pursued by the*
Murderers.]

Thou liest, thou shag-haired villain

Young fry of treachery!

He has killed me, mother

Why does Macduff flee the country? Was it
the right course of action?

In what ways might this scene be said to
differ from the rest of the play?

Scene 3

England. Before the King's palace. Enter **Malcolm**
and **Macduff.**

Malcolm   Let us seek out some desolate shade, and there
Weep our sad bosoms empty.

Macduff   Let us rather
Hold fast the mortal sword, and like good men
Bestride our down-fall'n birthdom: each new morn
New widows howl, new orphans cry, new sorrows   5
Strike heaven on the face, that it resounds
As if it felt with Scotland and yelled out
Like syllable of dolour.

Malcolm   What I believe, I'll wail;
What know, believe; and what I can redress,
As I shall find the time to friend, I will.   10
What you have spoke, it may be so perchance.
This tyrant, whose sole name blisters our tongues,
Was once thought honest: you have loved him well;
He hath not touched you yet. I am young, but something
You may deserve of him through me; and wisdom   15
To offer up a weak, poor, innocent lamb,
T'appease an angry god.

Macduff   I am not treacherous.

Malcolm   But Macbeth is.
A good and virtuous nature may recoil
In an imperial charge. But I shall crave your pardon;   20
That which you are, my thoughts cannot transpose:
Angels are bright still, though the brightest fell:
Though all things foul would wear the brows of grace,
Yet grace must still look so.

Macduff   I have lost my hopes.

Malcolm   Perchance even there where I did find my doubts.   25
Why in that rawness left you wife and child,

---

3   **mortal**   deadly
4   **Bestride . . . birthdom**   stand over our native
    country and defend it as one might do for a
    comrade fallen in battle
4–5   What is the effect of the repeated 'new'?
6   **that**   so that
8–17   What is Malcolm's attitude towards Macduff at this
    point? It may help to 'translate' what he says into
    appropriate modern English.
8   **Like . . . dolour**   similar cries of sorrow
    wail   bewail, lament
10   **to friend**   favourable
11   **perchance**   perhaps
12   **sole**   very
14   **He . . . yet**   Explain the dramatic irony.
14–15   **something . . . me**   you may gain something from
    Macbeth by betraying me to him
15   **wisdom**   it may be wise
16–17   What kind of imagery is this?
19–20   **recoil . . . charge**   step away (from goodness)
    under a royal command
    Why do you think Shakespeare used the word
    'charge'? What word in the previous line suggested
    it to him?
21   **my thoughts**   What thoughts?
    transpose   change, transform
22   **the brightest**   Lucifer (the devil), who fell from
    Heaven because of his pride and ambition
    How is he compared with Macbeth? Remember
    how the Porter referred to Macbeth's castle.
23   **would wear**   would like to appear to wear
24   **grace . . . so**   virtue must still appear as it is
26   **rawness**   unprotected situation

How, in lines 23–4, is Malcolm saying that it
is difficult to judge Macduff's intentions?

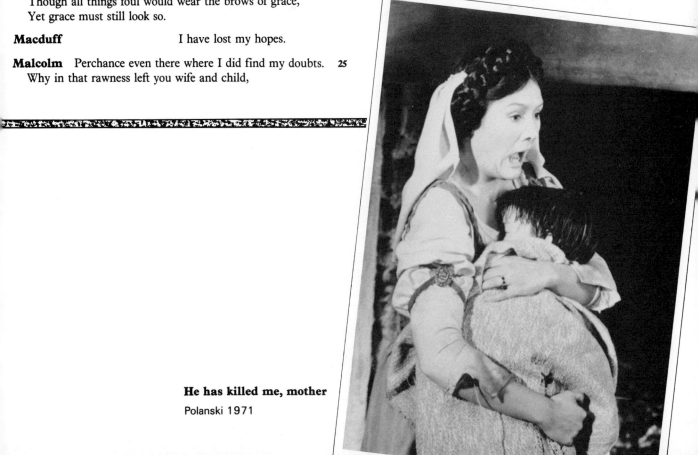

He has killed me, mother

Polanski 1971

27 motives influences
29 jealousies be your dishonours my suspicions be regarded as to you dishonour
30 mine own safeties as regard for my own safety
rightly just completely honest
32 basis foundation
33 goodness that is, the forces of right
check confront, call to account
34 affeered legally confirmed (that is, Macbeth's title to the crown)
37 to boot in addition
38 fear doubt, mistrust
41 withal also
42 right rightful claim to the throne
43 England Edward the Confessor, King of England The name of a country was often used as a direct reference to the ruling monarch. Why do you think this was so?
44 goodly representing (i) a considerable number; (ii) the forces of goodness
for despite
48 More suffer suffer more
49 What who
51 particulars particular kinds
grafted planted
52 opened as a bud opens into flower (continuing the horticultural image in the previous line)
55 confineless unlimited evil
57 top surpass, exceed

Spot two images derived from clothing on this page. To what effect are they used?

Those precious motives, those strong knots of love,
Without leave-taking? I pray you,
Let not my jealousies be your dishonours,
But mine own safeties: you may be rightly just,　　**30**
Whatever I shall think.

Macduff　　　　　　　　　Bleed, bleed, poor country!
Great tyranny, lay thou thy basis sure,
For goodness dares not check thee: wear thou thy wrongs,
The title is affeered! Fare thee well, lord:
I would not be the villain that thou think'st　　**35**
For the whole space that's in the tyrant's grasp,
And the rich East to boot.

Malcolm　　　　　　　　　Be not offended:
I speak not as in absolute fear of you:
I think our country sinks beneath the yoke,
It weeps, it bleeds, and each new day a gash　　**40**
Is added to her wounds. I think withal
There would be hands uplifted in my right;
And here from gracious England have I offer
Of goodly thousands. But for all this,
When I shall tread upon the tyrant's head,　　**45**
Or wear it on my sword, yet my poor country
Shall have more vices than it had before,
More suffer and more sundry ways than ever,
By him that shall succeed.

Macduff　　　　　　　　　What should he be?

Malcolm　It is myself I mean: in whom I know　　**50**
All the particulars of vice so grafted
That, when they shall be opened, black Macbeth
Will seem as pure as snow, and the poor state
Esteem him as a lamb, being compared
With my confineless harms.

Macduff　　　　　　　　　Not in the legions　　**55**
Of horrid hell can come a devil more damned
In evils to top Macbeth.

Macduff and director in rehearsal, RSC 1982

Malcolm   I grant him bloody,
Luxurious, avaricious, false, deceitful,
Sudden, malicious, smacking of every sin
That has a name: but there's no bottom, none,   60
In my voluptuousness: your wives, your daughters,
Your matrons and your maids, could not fill up
The cistern of my lust, and my desire
All continent impediments would o'erbear
That did oppose my will. Better Macbeth,   65
Than such an one to reign.

Macduff   Boundless intemperance
In nature is a tyranny; it hath been
Th'untimely emptying of the happy throne,
And fall of many kings. But fear not yet
To take upon you that is yours: you may   70
Convey your pleasures in a spacious plenty,
And yet seem cold, the time you may so hoodwink:
We have willing dames enough; there cannot be
That vulture in you, to devour so many
As will to greatness dedicate themselves,   75
Finding it so inclined.

Malcolm   With this there grows
In my most ill-composed affection such
A staunchless avarice that, were I king,
I should cut off the nobles for their lands,
Desire his jewels and this other's house,   80
And my more-having would be as a sauce
To make me hunger more, that I should forge
Quarrels unjust against the good and loyal,
Destroying them for wealth.

Macduff   This avarice
Sticks deeper: grows with more pernicious root   85
Than summer-seeming lust: and it hath been
The sword of our slain kings: yet do not fear;
Scotland hath foisons to fill up your will

58 **Luxurious** lustful
There is no evidence in the play that Macbeth is
lecherous or avaricious. So why does Malcolm say
this?
59 **Sudden** suddenly violent
61 **voluptuousness** lecherousness
Malcolm compares the endlessness of his lust with
a 'cistern' (line 63) which has no bottom.
64 **continent** restraining
    o'erbear break down, overpower
67 **nature** a man's nature
70 **that** that which
71 **Convey** secretly arrange
72 **cold** chaste, temperate
    time world, people
    hoodwink deceive
75 **greatness** that is, a king
76 **it** greatness (a king)
    With in addition to
77 **ill-composed affection** unbalanced character,
    evil nature
78 **staunchless** uncontrollable
79 **cut off** kill
80 **his** one man's
82 **forge** invent
86 **summer-seeming** like summer: (i) hot; (ii) short
    and passing
87 **sword** cause of death
    slain that is, murdered
88 **foisons** plenty, abundance

Why is Malcolm painting this evil picture of
himself?

But fear not yet
To take upon you that is yours
RSC 1976

89   mere own   own royal possessions
      All   that is, all these vices
      portable   bearable, tolerable
90   weighed   counter-balanced
93   Bounty   generosity
95   relish   How does this metaphor compare with
      'smacking' on line 59?
96   division   variations
      each several   every kind of
98   Why do you think milk is used as an image of
      plenty and peace?
99   Uproar   destroy
97–   Malcolm's self-accusation sums up precisely what
100   Macbeth has done.
104   untitled   illegal
107   interdiction   condemnation
108   blaspheme his breed   disgrace his family
110   that is, in prayer
111   Died . . . lived   (i) rejected all worldliness; (ii) was
      always prepared for death and heaven
112   upon   against (and in line 131)
113   breast   heart, which was considered the source of
      feelings
115   Child of integrity   born of your honest nature
116   scruples   suspicious
118   trains   tricks
119   modest . . . me   commonsense holds me back

Describe the part played in *Macbeth* by any
one of the **king-becoming graces** men-
tioned in lines 92–4.

What has Macduff unknowingly demon-
strated to Malcolm?

Rewrite in your own words lines 95–100.

Of your mere own. All these are portable,
With other graces weighed.   90

Malcolm   But I have none. The king-becoming graces,
As justice, verity, temp'rance, stableness,
Bounty, perseverance, mercy, lowliness,
Devotion, patience, courage, fortitude,
I have no relish of them, but abound   95
In the division of each several crime,
Acting it many ways. Nay, had I power, I should
Pour the sweet milk of concord into hell,
Uproar the universal peace, confound
All unity on earth.   100

Macduff   O Scotland! O Scotland!

Malcolm   If such a one be fit to govern, speak:
I am as I have spoken.

Macduff   Fit to govern!
No, not to live. O nation miserable!
With an untitled tyrant bloody-sceptred,
When shalt thou see thy wholesome days again,   105
Since that the truest issue of thy throne
By his own interdiction stands accused
And does blaspheme his breed? Thy royal father
Was a most sainted king; the queen that bore thee
Oft'ner upon her knees than on her feet,
Died every day she lived. Fare thee well!   110
These evils thou repeat'st upon thyself
Hath banished me from Scotland. O my breast,
Thy hope ends here!

Malcolm   Macduff, this noble passion,
Child of integrity, hath from my soul   115
Wiped the black scruples, reconciled my thoughts
To thy good truth and honour. Devilish Macbeth
By many of these trains hath sought to win me
Into his power; and modest wisdom plucks me
From over-credulous haste: but God above   120

**If such a one be fit to govern, speak:
I am as I have spoken**

National Theatre 1978

Deal between thee and me! for even now
I put myself to thy direction, and
Unspeak mine own detraction; her abjure
The taints and blames I laid upon myself,
For strangers to my nature. I am yet   125
Unknown to woman, never was forsworn,
Scarcely have coveted what was mine own,
At no time broke my faith, would not betray
The devil to his fellow, and delight
No less in truth than life: my first false speaking   130
Was this upon myself: what I am truly
Is thine and my poor country's to command:
Whither indeed, before they here-approach,
Old Siward, with ten thousand warlike men,
Already at a point, was setting forth.   135
Now we'll together, and the chance of goodness
Be like our warranted quarrel! Why are you silent?

Macduff Such welcome and unwelcome things at once
'Tis hard to reconcile.

[*Enter a* **Doctor**]

Malcolm Well, more anon. Comes the king forth, I pray   140
you?

Doctor Ay, sir: there are a crew of wretched souls
That stay his cure: their malady convinces
The great assay of art; but at his touch,
Such sanctity hath heaven given his hand,
They presently amend.

Malcolm   I thank you, doctor.   145

[*Exit* **Doctor**]

Macduff What's the disease he means?

Malcolm   'Tis called the Evil:
A most miraculous work in this good king,
Which often, since my here-remain in England,

---

121 **Deal ... me** guide our relationship
122 **to** under
123 **Unspeak ... detraction** take back what I spoke against myself
125 **For** as
126 **Unknown to woman** that is, sexually
     forsworn dishonoured by lying
131 **this** that is, the false accusations
133 **Whither** to that place
135 **at a point** ready for action
136 **we'll** we'll go (to Scotland)
136-7 **chance ... quarrel** may the chances of our success equal the justness of our cause
137 **Why are you silent?** Why *is* Macduff silent? What is he thinking? How might an actor convey this? Does the unfinished line 139 suggest another silence?
140 **the king** the English King, Edward the Confessor
141 **crew** crowd
142 **That stay** who await
     convinces defeats
143 **assay of art** efforts of medical science
145 **presently amend** immediately get well
146 **the Evil** scrofula, which was called 'the King's Evil' because it was reputed that English monarchs had the power of healing it
     Is Malcolm implying that the good king has other healing powers? Is Shakespeare flattering King James?

Rewrite in your own words lines 114–25 (**... to my nature**).

Why does the anonymous Doctor make his brief appearance? What does he tell us about the English King, and to what dramatic effect?

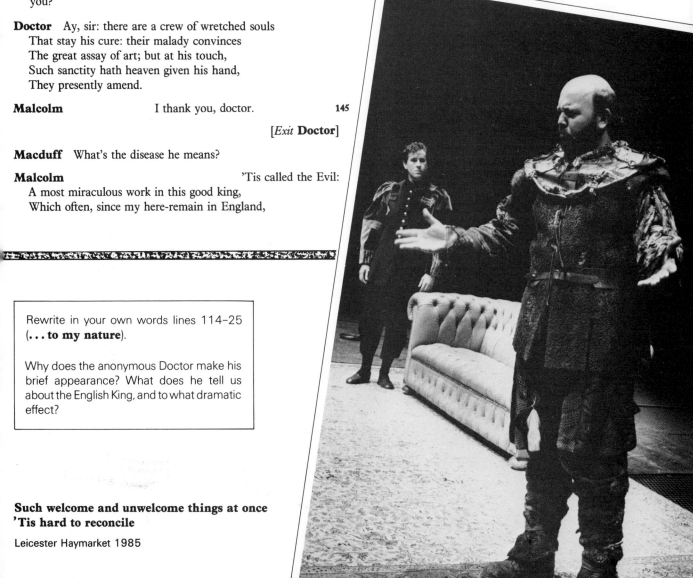

**Such welcome and unwelcome things at once
'Tis hard to reconcile**

Leicester Haymarket 1985

149   **solicits** gains help from
150   **strangely-visited** afflicted with unusual diseases
152   **mere** complete
153   **stamp** coin stamped with the image of an angel
King James continued the practice, but was so
frightened by the disease that he merely put the
coin around the necks of victims, refusing to cure
the 'evil' by touching them.
155   **leaves** bequeaths
156   **benediction** blessed gift
With in addition to
virtue power
158   **sundry** various
159   **speak him** proclaim him to be
160   Has Malcolm forgotten Ross (see Act I Scene 6)?
Or is he implying that he is suspicious of him
(which would be consistent with Malcolm's
behaviour in this scene)? Either way, how do you
think he can recognise Ross as a fellow Scot?
161   **gentle** noble
162   **betimes** quickly
164   **Stands Scotland where it did?** Actors have
found that this line sounds ridiculous. Practise
delivering it.
166   **mother** see the milk image in line 98
nothing nobody
167   **who** one who
169   **not marked** but not noticed – why not?
170   **modern ecstasy** commonplace emotion
170–1   **dead man's . . . who** Ross says that in Scotland
people scarcely bother to ask for whom the funeral
bell is tolling (because such an event is so
common).
173   **or ere they sicken** before they fall ill
relation story, report
174   **nice** elaborate, detailed

In the play we meet two kings and hear
about another. From what you have learned
from the play about the way they behave as
kings and from what you know about
Malcolm, what kind of king do you think
Shakespeare wants us to imagine *he* will
be?

Re-read this scene up to the entry of Ross.
With close reference to what Malcolm and
Macduff are discussing, show how important
their conversation is to the play as a
whole.

I have seen him do. How he solicits heaven,
Himself best knows: but strangely-visited people,   150
All swoln and ulcerous, pitiful to the eye,
The mere despair of surgery, he cures,
Hanging a golden stamp about their necks,
Put on with holy prayers: and 'tis spoken,
To the succeeding royalty he leaves   155
The healing benediction. With this strange virtue
He hath a heavenly gift of prophecy,
And sundry blessings hang about his throne
That speak him full of grace.

[*Enter* **Ross**]

Macduff   See, who comes here.

Malcolm   My countryman; but yet I know him not.   160

Macduff   My ever-gentle cousin, welcome hither.

Malcolm   I know him now: good God, betimes remove
The means that makes us strangers!

Ross   Sir, amen.

Macduff   Stands Scotland where it did?

Ross   Alas, poor country,
Almost afraid to know itself. It cannot   165
Be called our mother, but our grave; where nothing,
But who knows nothing, is once seen to smile;
Where sighs and groans and shrieks that rend the air,
Are made, not marked; where violent sorrow seems
A modern ecstasy: the dead man's knell   170
Is there scarce asked for who, and good men's lives
Expire before the flowers in their caps,
Dying or ere they sicken.

Macduff   O, relation
Too nice, and yet too true!

Malcolm   What's the newest grief?

The angel coin, see note line 15

Ross That of an hour's age doth hiss the speaker; 175
Each minute teems a new one.

Macduff   How does my wife?

Ross Why, well.

Macduff   And all my children?

Ross   Well too.

Macduff The tyrant has not battered at their peace?

Ross No, they were well at peace, when I did leave 'em.

Macduff Be not a niggard of your speech: how goes't? 180

Ross When I came hither to transport the tidings
Which I have heavily borne, there ran a rumour
Of many worthy fellows that were out;
Which was to my belief witnessed the rather,
For that I saw the tyrant's power a-foot. 185
Now is the time of help: your eye in Scotland
Would create soldiers, make our women fight,
To doff their dire distresses.

Malcolm   Be't their comfort
We are coming thither: gracious England hath
Lent us good Siward and then thousand men; 190
An older and a better soldier none
That Christendom gives out.

Ross   Would I could answer
This comfort with the like! But I have words,
That would be howled out in the desert air,
Where hearing should not latch them. 195

Macduff   What concern they?
The general cause? or is it a fee-grief
Due to some single breast?

Ross   No mind that's honest
But in it shares some woe, though the main part
Pertains to you alone.

175 a person reporting what happened an hour ago is hissed (because the news is stale)
176 **teems** gives birth to
177 **Well too** Ross does not perfectly complete the verse line. What dramatic effect does this give? Try saying the whole of their line with different people reading Ross and Macduff.
182 **rumour** What rumour, do you suppose?
182–8 Why does Ross turn to the general situation?
183 **out** risen in rebellion
184 **witnessed the rather** actually witnessed
185 **For that** because
       power army
186 **your eye** your (i) leadership; (ii) presence (in that men can see and be inspired by you)
188 **doff** cast off (another clothing image)
189 **gracious England** see line 43
191 **older** more experienced
       none there is none
192 **gives out** proclaims
194 **would** should
195 **latch** catch, latch onto
196–7 **fee-grief . . . breast** grief which is the private property of one person ('fee' is a legal metaphor, continued in 'Due to' and 'shares' in the following lines)
197 **No mind** there's no person

Rewrite, in clear modern English, lines 164–76.

How does my wife?
Young Vic 1984

202 **possess** put them in possession of
203 **Humh!** Shakespeare means to indicate any
     inarticulate gasp of alarm, although this looks weak
     on the page. Try saying it in order to suggest
     Macduff's dreadful foreboding. Can you suggest a
     better combination of letters on the page?
205 **manner** that is, of their deaths
206 **on the quarry** on top of the dead bodies (a
     hunting metaphor)
     deer Explain the pun.
208 What is Macduff doing?
210 **Whispers . . . heart** whispers to the overburdened
     heart
     Shakespeare is using an old proverb.
212 **must be from thence** had to be away from there
213– It was thought that one passion drove out another.
  15   Do Malcolm's words show a lack of imagination on
       the part of one who is not himself a father?
215 The verse line is unfinished. What does this
     suggest?
216 **He has no children** There are three possible
     interpretations of this remark: (i) Malcolm has no
     children – said to Ross as a comment on lines 213–
     15; (ii) Macbeth has no children (and thus I
     cannot take appropriate revenge); (iii) Macbeth has
     no children (if he had he would never have killed
     the children of others).
     Which interpretation do you prefer?
217 **hell-kite** see Act III Scene 4 line 74
219 **swoop** Why is this metaphor used? This is
     another incomplete verse line.
220 **Dispute** (i) face; (ii) fight against
222 **but remember** help remembering

Humh! I guess at it
RSC 1982

Macduff   If it be mine,
Keep it not from me, quickly let me have it.   200

Ross Let not your ears despise my tongue for ever,
Which shall possess them with the heaviest sound
That ever yet they heard.

Macduff   Humh! I guess at it.

Ross Your castle is surprised; your wife and babes
Savagely slaughtered: to relate the manner,   205
Were, on the quarry of these murdered deer,
To add the death of you.

Malcolm   Merciful heaven!
What, man! ne'er pull your hat upon your brows;
Give sorrow words: the grief that does not speak
Whispers the o'er-fraught heart and bids it break.   210

Macduff My children too?

Ross   Wife, children, servants, all
That could be found.

Macduff   And I must be from thence!
My wife killed too?

Ross   I have said.

Malcolm   Be comforted:
Let's make us med'cines of our great revenge,
To cure this deadly grief.   215

Macduff He has no children. All my pretty ones?
Did you say all? O, hell-kite! All?
What, all my pretty chickens and their dam
At one fell swoop?

Malcolm Dispute it like a man.   220

Macduff   I shall do so;
But I must also feel it as a man:
I cannot but remember such things were,

That were most precious to me. Did heaven look on,
And would not take their part? Sinful Macduff,
They were all struck for thee! naught that I am,   225
Not for their own demerits, but for mine,
Fell slaughter on their souls: heaven rest them now!

Malcolm   Be this the whetstone of your sword: let grief
Convert to anger; blunt not the heart, enrage it.

Macduff   O, I could play the woman with mine eyes,   230
And braggart with my tongue! But, gentle heavens,
Cut short all intermission; front to front
Bring thou this fiend of Scotland and myself;
Within my sword's length set him; if he 'scape,
Heaven forgive him too!

Malcolm   This tune goes manly.   235
Come, go we to the king: our power is ready,
Our lack is nothing but our leave. Macbeth
Is ripe for shaking, and the powers above
Put on their instruments. Receive what cheer you may;
The night is long that never finds the day.   240

[*Exeunt*]

225   **naught**   wicked
What modern word do you think derives from 'naught'?

228–9   see note to lines 213–15

230   What does he mean?

231   **And . . . tongue**   that is, spend time boasting of what he will do

232   **intermission**   interval, delay
front to front   face to face (literally, forehead to forehead)

235   **too**   either (i) because (if I let him escape) my wish for revenge will have cooled; or (ii) as well as me, for letting him escape

235   **This . . . manly**   this is a manly strain in which to speak

237   **Our lack . . . leave**   we need only say goodbye (to the king, possibly)

238   **shaking**   that is, as fruit from a tree

239   **Put on their instruments**   either (i) arm themselves; or (ii) urge on (us) their instruments of revenge.
Line 239 is called an 'alexandrine'. Can you see how its rhythm differs from the usual verse lines (pentameters) of the play?

240   How is this imagery appropriate to the play?

Act IV Scene 3 is often regarded as tedious, and it was heavily cut in the Polanski film version of *Macbeth*. Try to cut it down. Then compare your version with the original. What has been gained? What lost?

Show how the confrontation between good and evil is built up (a) in Act IV Scene 3, and (b) in the play as a whole.

How is Shakespeare setting up Macduff as Macbeth's legitimate killer/executioner?

Write director's notes on Act IV Scene 3 for the actor playing Macduff.

What is Malcolm's view of 'a man'?

**O, I could play the woman with mine eyes,
And braggard with my tongue!**

National Theatre 1978

SD Physic medicine
   He is a physician.
3 field that is, battlefield (against the rebels 'that
   were out')
4 night-gown dressing gown
   Elizabethans slept naked. In Roman Polanski's film
   of *Macbeth*, Lady Macbeth was naked. Is this
   appropriate? Is it distracting? What is this scene
   about?
5 closet writing cabinet, or chest in which valuables
   were kept
8 perturbation upset, disorder, reversal
   How does Lady Macbeth's behaviour as described
   here fit a repeated motif in the play?
9 effects of watching actions of one who is awake
10 slumbery agitation sleep-walking
10-11 actual/performances actions
12 after her according to what she said
13 meet appropriate, advisable
14-15 Pretend that you are the Gentlewoman, and explain
   to a close friend as fully as possible why you will
   not report Lady Macbeth 'after her' to the Doctor.
16 Lo look
   her very guise the way she has done it before
17 close hidden
19-20 Why does Lady Macbeth want light by her always?
   See Act I Scene 5 lines 49-50, and comment on
   the horrible irony of the contrast.

Act V

Scene 1

Dunsinane. A room in the castle. Enter a **Doctor of Physic,**
and a **Waiting Gentlewoman.**

Doctor   I have two nights watched with you, but can perceive
no truth in your report. When was it she last walked?

Gentlewoman   Since his majesty went into the field, I have
seen her rise from her bed, throw her night-gown upon her,
unlock her closet, take forth paper, fold it, write upon't, read   5
it, afterwards seal it, and again return to bed; yet all this while
in a most fast sleep.

Doctor   A great perturbation in nature, to receive at once the
benefit of sleep and do the effects of watching! In this
slumbery agitation, besides her walking and other actual   10
performances, what, at any time, have you heard her say?

Gentlewoman   That, sir, which I will not report after her.

Doctor   You may to me, and 'tis most meet you should.

Gentlewoman   Neither to you nor any one, having no witness
to confirm my speech.   15

[*Enter* **Lady Macbeth,** *with a taper*]

Lo you, here she comes! This is her very guise, and upon my
life fast asleep. Observe her, stand close.

Doctor   How came she by that light?

Gentlewoman   Why, it stood by her: she has light by her
continually; 'tis her command.   20

Doctor   You see, her eyes are open.

Gentlewoman   Ay, but their sense are shut.

Enter **Lady Macbeth,** *with a taper*
National Theatre 1978

> Why do you think the scene is introduced by
> the Doctor and Gentlewoman in prose? Can
> you spot the line where the Doctor slips into
> verse?

Doctor   What is it she does now? Look, how she rubs her
hands.

Gentlewoman   It is an accustomed action with her, to seem   25
thus washing her hands: I have known her continue in this a
quarter of an hour.

Lady Macbeth   Yet here's a spot.

Doctor   Hark, she speaks! I will set down what comes from
her, to satisfy my remembrance the more strongly.   30

Lady Macbeth   Out, damned spot! out, I say! One; two: why,
then 'tis time to do't. Hell is murky! Fie, my lord, fie! a
soldier, and afeard? What need we fear who knows it, when
none can call out power to accompt? Yet who would have
thought the old man to have had so much blood in him?   35

Doctor   Do you mark that?

Lady Macbeth   The Thane of Fife had a wife; where is she
now? What, will these hands ne'er be clean? No more o'that,
my lord, no more o'that: you mar all with this starting.

Doctor   Go to, to to; you have known what you should not.   40

Gentlewoman   She has spoke what she should not, I am sure
of that: heaven knows what she has known.

Lady Macbeth   Here's the smell of the blood still: all the
perfumes of Arabia will not sweeten this little hand. Oh! oh!
oh!   45

Doctor   What a sigh is there! The heart is sorely charged.

Gentlewoman   I would not have such a heart in my bosom, for
the dignity of the whole body.

Doctor   Well, well, well –

Gentlewoman   Pray God it be, sir.   50

Doctor   This disease is beyond my practice: yet I have known
those which have walked in their sleep who have died holily in
their beds.

28   How is this ironic when contrasted with what she
said in Act II Scene 2?
29   **set**   write
31   **One; two**   Of what is she thinking?
32   Where does she imagine that she now is?
34   **accompt**   account
36   **mark**   notice
37   **Fife . . . wife**   What effect does the 'nursery rhyme'
style have on you?
39   What past event(s) are in her mind now? Find an
earlier instance where Lady Macbeth used a word
similar to 'starting'.
40   **Go to**   now then
43–4   Compare with her husband at Act II Scene 2 lines
60–3.
46   **sorely charged**   heavily laden
48   **dignity**   worth, rank, well-being
50   The Gentlewoman is playing upon the Doctor's
words – Shakespeare gives scope even to such a
small part.
51   **practice**   skill, art

> **I think but dare not speak** (line 71).
> Bearing in mind that the Doctor has been
> taking notes (see lines 29–30), imagine that
> you are the Doctor. Jot down those notes
> (you would not have time to write much).
> Then go away and write a frank but con-
> fidential report on your patient's condition.

Leicester Haymarket 1985

56   on's of his
57   Even so How does the Doctor say this? What is he thinking?
59-60   what's . . . undone Compare with Act III Scene 2 line 12.
63   Foul . . . abroad Horrible rumours are going about.
66   divine priest (to cure her soul)
68   annoyance injury
      What does the Doctor fear?
69   still constantly
70   mated baffled

When did we last see Lady Macbeth before this scene? Discuss in what ways she has changed.

Write down whatever you suppose Lady Macbeth wrote when she rose from her bed (lines 3–7).

Why do you think this scene is written entirely in prose?

To what events does Lady Macbeth refer which have taken place earlier in the play? Be specific, and quote line references.

Lady Macbeth Wash your hands, put on your night-gown, look not so pale: I tell you yet again, Banquo's buried; he   55
cannot come out on's grave.

Doctor Even so?

Lady Macbeth To bed, to bed: there's knocking at the gate: come, come, come, come, give me your hand: what's done, cannot be undone: to bed, to bed, to bed.   60

[*Exit*]

Doctor Will she go now to bed?

Gentlewoman Directly.

Doctor Foul whisp'rings are abroad: unnatural deeds
Do breed unnatural troubles: infected minds
To their deaf pillows will discharge their secrets: 65
More needs she the divine than the physician:
God, God forgive us all! Look after her,
Remove from her the means of all annoyance,
And still keep eyes upon her. So, good night:
My mind she has mated and amazed my sight: 70
I think, but dare not speak.

Gentlewoman   Good night, good doctor.

[*Exeunt*]

RSC 1982

Scene 2

The country near Dunsinane. Drum and colours. Enter
Menteith, Caithness, Angus, Lennox, *and* **Soldiers.**

Menteith   The English power is near, led on by Malcolm,
His uncle Siward and the good Macduff.
Revenges burn in them: for their dear causes
Would to the bleeding and the grim alarm
Excite the mortified man.

Angus   Near Birnam wood   5
Shall we meet them, and that way are they coming.

Caithness   Who knows if Donalbain be with his brother?

Lennox   For certain, sir, he is not: I have a file
Of all the gentry: there is Siward's son,
And many unrough youths, that even now   10
Protest their first of manhood.

Monteith   What does the tyrant?

Caithness   Great Dunsinane he strongly fortifies:
Some say he's mad; others, that lesser hate him,
Do call it valiant fury: but, for certain,
He cannot buckle his distempered cause   15
Within the belt of rule.

Angus   Now does he feel
His secret murders sticking on his hands;
Now minutely revolts upbraid his faith-breach;
Those he commands move only in command,
Nothing in love: now does he feel his title   20
Hang loose about him, like a giant's robe
Upon a dwarfish thief.

Menteith   Who then shall blame
His pestered senses to recoil and start,
When all that is within him does condemn
Itself for being there?

SD   These are the 'false thanes' to which Macbeth refers in the next scene. Here we see that it is not simply an English army which is helping Malcolm to defeat a Scottish force, but a union of Anglo-Scottish forces which are combining against treason. What may have been the topical relevance of this in the early years of the seventeenth century?
colours   military banners
1   **power**   army
3   **dear**   heartfelt
4   **bleeding . . . alarm**   that is, the battlefield
5   **mortified**   dead
     Birnam wood   What drama is in these words? What sense of anticipation do they generate in the audience?
8   **file**   list (see Act III Scene 1 line 94)
10   **unrough**   smooth-cheeked, beardless
11   **Protest . . . of**   proclaim the first signs of their
15   **distempered**   bloated, sick
15-16   **buckle . . . rule**   The idea is that Macbeth can no longer control either his subjects or his own passions.
16-17   **Now . . . hands**   see Act II Scene 2 lines 60-3
18   Now every minute rebellions censure his treachery.
19   **in command**   because under orders
20-2   How does this metaphor follow on from lines 15-16, and fit into a pattern of imagery in the play? See Act I Scene 3 lines 144-6 and Act I Scene 7 lines 32-6.
23   **pestered**   troubled
     In what way can we say that Menteith perfectly understands Macbeth's state of mind?

> now does he feel his title
> **Hang loose about him, like a giant's**
>   **robe**
> **Upon a dwarfish thief**
> Crucible Theatre 1985

27 **med'cine** probably meaning 'doctor' (what is the French for 'doctor'?); that is, Malcolm
   sickly weal diseased country
28 **in...purge** in order to cleanse our country
29 **Each drop** every part (with the implication that they will shed their last drop of blood to restore their country)
30 **dew** water and nourish
   sovereign (i) royal; (ii) supremely healing
   flower that is, Malcolm
   weeds that is, Macbeth and his followers

Caithness   Well, march we on,   25
To give obedience where 'tis truly owed:
Meet we the med'cine of the sickly weal,
And with him pour we, in our country's purge,
Each drop of us.

Lennox   Or so much as it needs
To dew the sovereign flower and drown the weeds.   30
Make we our march towards Birnam.

                                        [*Exeunt, marching*]

Leicester Haymarket 1985

Scene 3

Dunsinane. A room in the castle. Enter **Macbeth, Doctor,**
and **Attendants.**

Macbeth   Bring me no more reports, let them fly all:
Till Birnam wood remove to Dunsinane
I cannot taint with fear. What's the boy Malcolm?
Was he not born of woman? The spirits that know
All mortal consequence have pronounced me thus: 5
'Fear not, Macbeth, no man that's born of woman
Shall e'er have power upon thee'. Then fly, false thanes,
And mingle with the English epicures:
The mind I sway by and the heart I bear
Shall never sag with doubt nor shake with fear.   10

[*Enter a* **Servant**]

The devil damn thee black, thou cream-faced loon!
Where got'st thou that goose look?

Servant   There is ten thousand –

Macbeth   Geese, villain?

Servant   Soldiers, sir.

Macbeth   Go prick thy face and over-red thy fear,
Thou lily-livered boy. What soldiers, patch?   15
Death of thy soul! those linen cheeks of thine
Are counsellors to fear. What soldiers, whey-face?

Servant   The English force, so please you.

Macbeth   Take thy face hence.

[*Exit* **Servant**]

Seyton! – I am sick at heart
When I behold – Seyton, I say! – This push   20
Will cheer me ever, or disseat me now.

1 **them**   his thanes
   fly   run away, desert
3 **taint**   become infected
5 **All mortal consequence**   the destiny of all
   humans
8 **epicures**   luxury-loving people
   Does this reveal a Scottish attitude towards
   Southerners?
9 **I sway by**   by which I control myself and my
   actions
11 **cream-faced**   How many more references can you
   find on this page to the Servant's paleness?
   loon   rogue
15 It was supposed that courage came from the liver.
   patch   clown
17 **Are counsellors**   encourage others
20 **push**   critical attack
21 **cheer**   a pun, meaning (i) cheer me up, (ii) keep
   me on the throne ('cheer' and 'chair' were
   pronounced the same way in Elizabethan English)
   disseat   unseat (from the throne)

What Macbeth says and does is now wild,
yet he retains a tragically ironic faith in what
the witches have said and this gives him,
paradoxically, a desperate confidence.

How does the rhythm of his lines help to
reveal his mental state?

Young Vic 1984

22 way course
23 sere withered
27 mouth-honour lip-service
28 fain rather, like to, gladly
22–8 Do you have any sympathy for Macbeth here? If so, why? Is he a sympathetic figure elsewhere in this scene, or in Act V as a whole?
31 What, do you suppose, 'was reported'?
37 In some productions the Doctor does not enter until this point. Where would you have him enter?
40 minister to treat
Is Macbeth's question a fair one? Is the Doctor's reply a fair one?
42 erase the troubles imprinted on the mind
43 oblivious causing forgetfulness
44 stuffed overburdened

I have lived long enough: my way of life
Is fall'n into the sere, the yellow leaf,
And that which should accompany old age,
As honour, love, obedience, troops of friends,   25
I must not look to have; but, in their stead,
Curses, not loud but deep, mouth-honour, breath
Which the poor heart would fain deny and dare not.
Seyton!

[*Enter* **Seyton**]

Seyton   What is your gracious pleasure?   30

Macbeth   What news more?

Seyton   All is confirmed, my lord, which was reported.

Macbeth   I'll fight, till from my bones my flesh be hacked.
Give me my armour.

Seyton   'Tis not needed yet.

Macbeth   I'll put it on.
Send out more horses, skirr the country round,   35
Hang those talk of fear. Give me mine armour.
How goes your patient, Doctor?

Doctor   Not so sick, my lord,
As she is troubled with thick-coming fancies,
That keep her from her rest.

Macbeth   Cure her of that:
Canst thou not minister to a mind diseased,   40
Pluck from the memory a rooted sorrow,
Raze out the written troubles of the brain,
And with some sweet oblivious antidote
Cleanse the stuffed bosom of that perilous stuff
Which weighs upon the heart?

Doctor   Therein the patient   45
Must minister to himself.

Royal Lyceum 1986

What is ironic about the name of Macbeth's most trusted servant?

Examine closely Macbeth's soliloquy (lines 19–29), and discuss the dramatic function of it. How is a soliloquy useful in putting over to an audience what dialogue cannot do?

Macbeth   Throw physic to the dogs, I'll none of it.
Come, put mine armour on; give me my staff;
Seyton, send out; Doctor, the thanes fly from me;
Come sir, dispatch. – If thou couldst, Doctor, cast   50
The water of my land, find her disease,
And purge it to a sound and pristine health,
I would applaud thee to the very echo
That should applaud again. – Pull't off, I say. –
What rhubarb, senna, or what purgative drug,   55
Would scour these English hence? Hear'st thou of them?

Doctor   Ay, my good lord; your royal preparation
Makes us hear something.

Macbeth   Bring it after me.
I will not be afraid of death and bane
Till Birnam forest come to Dunsinane.   60

[*Exeunt* **Macbeth** *and* **Seyton**]

Doctor   Were I from Dunsinane away and clear,
Profit again should hardly draw me here.

[*Exit*]

47   **physic**   medical skill
48   **staff**   either (i) general's baton; or (ii) spear
50   **dispatch**   hurry
50-1   **cast/The water**   analyse the urine (Scotland is the patient)
52   **purge**   cleanse, cure, heal
     What does this echo from the previous scene? In what way is it ironic?
54   **Pull't off**   refers to some part of Macbeth's armour
55   He refers to various laxatives which will purge the system of his country.
56   **scour**   cleanse
57-8   What is the tone of the Doctor's reply? Practise saying it in order to bring out that tone.
58   **it**   refers to part of Macbeth's armour (see line 54)
59   **bane**   destruction, ruin
60   Comment on the irony.
62   **Profit**   money

Suppose that Seyton has been Macbeth's body-servant for some time. Imagine that you are Seyton. Say what changes you have observed in your master since he became king, and what your thoughts and feelings about him are as you help him to arm.

Either: Write a report on Macbeth's state of mind as if you are the Doctor.
Or: Discuss Macbeth's state of mind bearing in mind *all* you know. (N.B. You will know more than the Doctor.)
Or: Write a letter from the Doctor to his wife explaining why he has been delayed at Dunsinane.

New Victoria Theatre 1976

SD All the Scottish thanes whom we have previously seen in the play are shown to have deserted Macbeth.

2 **chambers will be safe** bedrooms shall be safe places
In what way was this not so earlier in the play?
nothing not at all

5 **shadow** conceal

6 **host** army
discovery intelligence, reconnaissance scouts (of the enemy)

8 **no other but** nothing except that
Why is Macbeth so 'confident'?

9 **still in** constantly inside

9–10 **endure ... before't** allow us to besiege it

11 **advantage** opportunity

12 both great men and ordinary people have rebelled against him

14 **censures** judgments

15 **Attend ... event** wait until the actual situation is made clear
Why does Macduff say this? Contrast him as a soldier with Malcolm.

17 **due decision** certainty

18 **owe** actually possess

19 speculation can only give rise to uncertain hopes

20 but the actual outcome must be decided by fighting

21 **which** which outcome
war that is, army

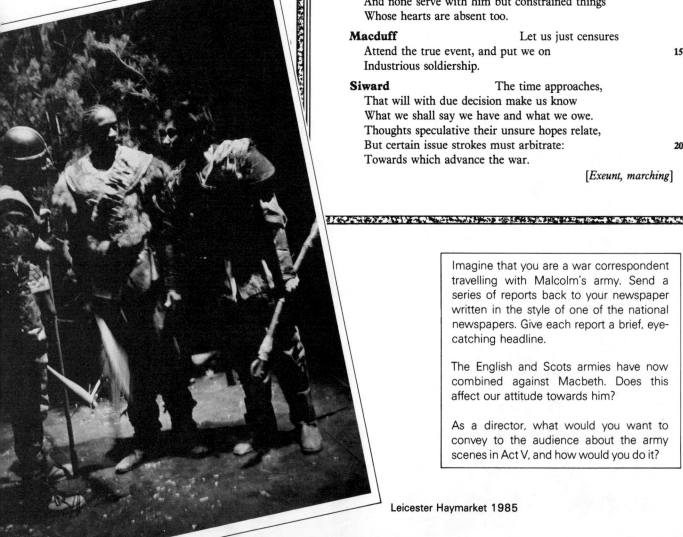

Scene 4

Country near Birnam Wood. Drum and colours. Enter
Malcolm, Siward, Macduff, Siward's son, Menteith, Caithness, Angus, Lennox, Ross *and* **Soldiers,** *marching.*

Malcolm　　Cousins, I hope, the days are near at hand
That chambers will be safe.

Menteith　　　　　　　　　We doubt it nothing.

Siward　What wood is this before us?

Menteith　　　　　　　　　　The wood of Birnam.

Malcolm　Let every soldier hew him down a bough,
And bear't before him: thereby shall we shadow 　5
The numbers of our host, and make discovery
Err in report of us.

Soldier　　　　　　It shall be done.

Siward　We learn no other but the confident tyrant
Keeps still in Dunsinane, and will endure
Our setting down before't.

Malcolm　　　　　　　　'Tis his main hope: 　10
For where there is advantage to be gone,
Both more and less have given him the revolt,
And none serve with him but constrained things
Whose hearts are absent too.

Macduff　　　　　　　Let us just censures
Attend the true event, and put we on 　15
Industrious soldiership.

Siward　　　　　　　The time approaches,
That will with due decision make us know
What we shall say we have and what we owe.
Thoughts speculative their unsure hopes relate,
But certain issue strokes must arbitrate: 　20
Towards which advance the war.

[Exeunt, marching]

Imagine that you are a war correspondent travelling with Malcolm's army. Send a series of reports back to your newspaper written in the style of one of the national newspapers. Give each report a brief, eye-catching headline.

The English and Scots armies have now combined against Macbeth. Does this affect our attitude towards him?

As a director, what would you want to convey to the audience about the army scenes in Act V, and how would you do it?

Leicester Haymarket 1985

Scene 5

Dunsinane. Within the castle. Enter **Macbeth, Seyton,** *and* **Soldiers** *with drum and colours.*

Macbeth Hang out our banners on the outward walls;
The cry is still 'They come': our castle's strength
Will laugh a siege to scorn: here let them lie
Till famine and the ague eat them up:
Were they not forced with those that should be ours,   5
We might have met them dareful, beard to beard,
And beat them backward home.

[*A cry of women within*]

What is that noise?

Seyton It is the cry of women, my good lord.

[*Exit*]

Macbeth I have almost forgot the taste of fears:
The time has been, my senses would have cooled   10
To hear a night-shriek, and my fell of hair
Would at a dismal treatise rouse and stir
As life were in't: I have supped full with horrors;
Direness, familiar to my slaughterous thoughts,
Cannot once start me.

[*Re-enter* **Seyton**]

Wherefore was that cry?   15

Seyton The queen, my lord, is dead.

Macbeth She should have died hereafter;
There would have been a time for such a word.
To-morrow, and to-morrow, and to-morrow,
Creeps in this pretty pace from day to day,   20

At the beginning of this scene Macbeth seems to be **the confident tyrant** (see line 8 of the previous scene). Discuss how he deteriorates during the scene. Is he aware of what is happening to him? Does he show bravery or rashness at the end of the scene?

1 Why do you think this order is given?
3 **them lie** the enemy settle down and besiege us
4 **ague** fever
5 **forced** reinforced
6 **dareful** boldly on the battlefield
10 **cooled** frozen
11 **night-shriek** the cry of an owl
    fell of hair scalp
12 **dismal treatise** tale of horror
13 **supped** Does this word remind you of other murders in the play?
14 **Direness** horrors
15 **once start me** startle me ever again
    Where else in the play has the word 'start' been used? Find it.
17 **should** either (i) would; or (ii) ought to Which do you prefer? (Look at line 18 before deciding.)
    hereafter after this
19 How does the rhythm of this line reinforce the feeling behind it?
20 **pretty pace** very slow speed

RSC 1986

21 recorded time (i) an individual's history (that is, his life); (ii) the history of the world
23 dusty death death, when a body crumbles into dust
candle What does the candle symbolise? What might Macbeth do at this moment? (See the Bible, Job 18:6.)
24 shadow see the Bible, Job 8:9 and Psalms 39:7 and note to Act IV Scene 1 line 111
poor In what two senses might the actor be considered 'poor'?
28 What is the dramatic effect of the incomplete line?
33 watch guard
36 endure suffer
39 next nearest
40 cling shrivel, wither
sooth truth
41 as much that is, hang me
42 pull in resolution rein/hold back my confidence and determination
Where does the metaphor come from?
43 doubt suspect
equivocation double meaning (see Act I Scene 3 lines 123-6 and Act II Scene 3 lines 7-10)
47 avouches does appear alleges is shown to be fact
48 it makes no difference if we run away or remain here
49 'gin begin

OUT, OUT, BRIEF CANDLE!
SIR LAURENCE OLIVIER in MACBETH

To the last syllable of recorded time;
And all our yesterdays have lighted fools
The way to dusty death. Out, out, brief candle!
Life's but a walking shadow, a poor player
That struts and frets his hour upon the stage,   25
And then is heard no more: it is a tale
Told by an idiot, full of sound and fury,
Signifying nothing.

[*Enter a* **Messenger**]

Thou com'st to use thy tongue; thy story quickly.

Messenger Gracious my lord,   30
I should report that which I say I saw,
But know not how to do't.

Macbeth   Well, say, sir.

Messenger As I did stand my watch upon the hill,
I looked toward Birnam, and anon, methought
The wood began to move.

Macbeth   Liar and slave!   35

Messenger Let me endure your wrath, if't be not so:
Within this three mile may you see it coming.
I say, a moving grove.

Macbeth   If thou speak'st false,
Upon the next tree shalt thou hang alive,
Till famine cling thee: if thy speech be sooth,   40
I care not if thou dost for me as much.
I pull in resolution, and begin
To doubt th'equivocation of the fiend
That lies like truth: 'Fear not, till Birnam wood
Do come to Dunsinane'; and now a wood   45
Comes toward Dunsinane. Arm, arm, and out!
If this which he avouches does appear,
There is nor flying hence nor tarrying here.
I'gin to be aweary of the sun,

Learn lines 19-28; then write them out; then act them out as if for an audition for the part of Macbeth.

In order to help you to understand the lines fully you could attempt to rewrite them in modern English.

Sir Lawrence Olivier as Macbeth,
Stratford 1955
by Ruskin Spear RA

And wish th'estate o'th' world were now undone. 50
Ring the alarum bell! Blow, wind! come, wrack!
At least we'll die with harness on our back.

[*Exeunt*]

50 th'estate . . . undone the orderly condition of the whole universe were brought to chaos
51 wrack ruin, destruction (see Act IV Scene 1 lines 50–61)
52 harness armour (see the Bible, I Kings 22:34) What might have happened had Macbeth stayed in his castle? (Look back at the opening lines of this scene.)

Plan the lighting plot for this scene.

What is the dramatic effect of the build-up of short scenes alternating between within and without the castle?

How does Malcolm's leadership contrast with that of Macbeth?

At least we'll die with harness on our back
RSC 1982

1 **leavy** leafy
2 **show like those** appear like the soldiers that
uncle see Act V Scene 2 line 2
4 **battle** battalion
we Why does Malcolm not say 'I'?
5 **do** be done
6 **order** plan
7 **Do we but** if only we
power forces
8 **fight** that is, fight well
10 **harbingers** heralds, forerunners

Scene 6

Dunsinane. Before the castle gate. Drum and colours. Enter
Malcolm, Siward, Macduff, *and their army, with boughs.*

Malcolm   Now near enough: your leavy screens throw down,
And show like those you are. You, worthy uncle,
Shall with my cousin your right-noble son
Lead our first battle: worthy Macduff and we
Shall take upon's what else remains to do,   5
According to our order.

Siward   Fare you well.
Do we but find the tyrant's power to-night,
Let us be beaten, if we cannot fight.

Macduff   Make all our trumpets speak; give them all breath,
Those clamorous harbingers of blood and death.   10

[*Exeunt*]

They have tied me to a stake; I cannot fly

RSC 1988

DUNSINANE

Scene 7

Another part of the battlefield.

Macbeth They have tied me to a stake; I cannot fly,
But bear-like I must fight the course. What's he
That was not born of woman? Such a one
Am I to fear, or none.

[*Enter* **Young Siward**]

Young Siward What is thy name?

Macbeth   Thou'lt be afraid to hear it. **5**

Young Siward No; though thou call'st thyself a hotter name
Than any is in hell.

Macbeth   My name's Macbeth.

Young Siward The devil himself could not pronounce a title
More hateful to mine ear.

Macbeth   No, nor more fearful;

Young Siward Thou liest, abhorrèd tyrant; with my sword **10**
I'll prove the lie thou speak'st.

[*They fight, and* **Young Siward** *is slain*]

Macbeth   Thou wast born of woman.
But swords I smile at, weapons laugh to scorn,
Brandished by man that's of a woman born.

[*Exit. Alarums. Enter* **Macduff**]

Macduff That way the noise is. Tyrant, show thy face!
If thou be'est slain and with no stroke of mine, **15**
My wife and children's ghosts will haunt me still.
I cannot strike at wretched kerns, whose arms
Are hired to bear their staves; either thou, Macbeth,

Some editors break the rest of the play into two or three scenes; but it seems best to show that everybody is now outside the castle in a struggle which leads up to the climax and resolution of the play.

1-2 The bearbaiting pit was situated within earshot of the Globe Theatre, and the audience of the time would have found vivid this metaphor of a bear tied to a stake, attempting to fight off a series of attacks ('course') by dogs. See *King Lear*, Act III Scene 7 line 54 and page 52.

11 **born of woman** see the Bible, Job 14:1 and also the Burial Service ('Man that is born of woman hath but a short time to live . . .')
16 **still** forever
17 **kerns** mercenaries (see Act I Scene 2 line 13)
18 **staves** spear-shafts

> Why is the death of Young Siward dramatically necessary?

20   **undeeded**   unused, with no deeds performed
This is typical of Shakespeare's habit of coining
verbs from nouns.
There thou shouldst be   that's where you are
likely to be
22   **bruited**   announced (by the noise)
24   **gently rendered**   surrendered after no fierce
opposition
27   The victory is almost won.
29   **beside us**   on our side
30-1   In defeat an honourable Roman often committed
suicide by falling upon his own sword (e.g. Cato,
Brutus, Antony).
31-2   **whiles . . . them**   While I can see enemies, the
wounds are better inflicted upon them.
35   **thine**   your family
Is Macbeth showing a sign of remorse?
37   **terms**   words

Or else my sword with an unbattered edge
I sheathe again undeeded. There thou shouldst be;   20
By this great clatter, one of greatest note
Seems bruited. Let me find him, fortune!
And more I beg not.

[**Malcolm** *and* **Siward** *come up*]

Siward   This way, my lord; the castle's gently rendered:
The tyrant's people on both sides do fight,   25
The noble thanes do bravely in the war,
The day almost itself professes yours,
And little is to do.

Malcolm   We have met with foes
That strike beside us.

Siward   Enter, sir, the castle.

[*Exeunt*]

[**Macbeth** *returns*]

Macbeth   Why should I play the Roman fool, and die   30
On mine own sword? whiles I see lives, the gashes
Do better upon them.

[*Enter* **Macduff**]

Macduff   Turn, hell-hound, turn.

Macbeth   Of all men else I have avoided thee:
But get thee back, my soul is too much charged
With blood of thine already.   35

Macduff   I have no words:
My voice is in my sword, thou bloodier villain
Than terms can give thee out!

[*They fight*]

Plan the sound plot for this scene.

Macduff: **Turn, hell-hound, turn**
Macbeth: **Of all men else I have avoided
thee**

Leicester Haymarket 1985

Macbeth   Thou losest labour.
  As easy mayst thou the intrenchant air
  With thy keen sword impress as make me bleed:
  Let fall thy blade on vulnerable crests,   40
  I bear a charmed life, which must not yield
  To one of woman born.

Macduff   Despair thy charm,
  And let the angel whom thou still hast served
  Tell thee, Macduff was from his mother's womb
  Untimely ripped.   45

Macbeth   Accursed be that tongue that tells me so,
  For it hath cow'd my better part of man!
  And be these juggling fiends no more believed,
  That palter with us in a double sense,
  That keep the word of promise to our ear,   50
  And break it to our hope. I'll not fight with thee.

Macduff   Then yield thee, coward,
  And live to be the show and gaze o'th' time.
  We'll have thee, as our rarer monsters are,
  Painted upon a pole, and underwrit,   55
  'Here may you see the tyrant'.

Macbeth   I will not yield,
  To kiss the ground before young Malcolm's feet,
  And to be baited with the rabble's curse.
  Though Birnam wood be come to Dunsinane,
  And thou opposed, being of no woman born,   60
  Yet I will try the last. Before my body
  I throw my warlike shield: lay on, Macduff,
  And damned be him that first cries 'Hold, enough'.

[*Exeunt, fighting*]

[*Retreat and flourish. Enter, with drum and colours,*
Malcolm, Siward, Ross, Thanes *and* **Soldiers**.]

38 **intrenchant** uncuttable
39 **impress** make an impact upon
40 **crests** helmets
41 **must** can
42 **Despair** despair of
43 **angel . . . served** To whom do you think Macduff
  is referring?
  still constantly, always
45 **untimely** prematurely
47 **cow'd . . . man** crushed my manly spirit
48 **juggling** cheating, deceiving
49 who trick us by saying things which have a double
  meaning (see Act I Scene 3 lines 123–6, and
  comment on the irony)
60 **opposed** opposed to me
61 **try the last** that is, fight to the death
62 **lay on** attack

> Jot down director's notes for lines 35–63
> commenting particularly on movement and
> how you would like the lines delivered.

Oxford Playhouse 1982

64 we miss who are missing
65 go off exit from the stage; that is, be killed
      these the number of men here
67 your noble son Young Siward
68 a soldier's debt that is, the giving of his life
71 unshrinking station where he fought the post
      where he fought without shrinking
77 hairs pun on 'heirs'
      This kind of punning in a serious situation was quite
      acceptable to an Elizabethan audience. Look back
      in the text and see if you can find any comparable
      puns early in the play.
79 And . . . knolled and having said this, I have
      carried out the formality of acknowledging his
      death, as if by the tolling of his funeral bell
81 parted departed, died
      paid his score settled his debts (by doing his
      duty as a soldier, see line 68)
84 time see Act I Scene 5 line 62 and Act IV Scene
      3 line 72
85 compassed surrounded, encircled
      pearl nobility; but probably with a secondary
      suggestion of the precious stones in a crown
      Should the crown have been transferred to
      Malcolm's head by this point? Write director's notes
      for the staging of this final page of text.
86 who are thinking what I am saying
      salutation greeting

Malcolm   I would the friends we miss were safe arrived.

Siward   Some must go off: and yet, by these I see,   **65**
So great a day as this is cheaply bought.

Malcolm   Macduff is missing, and your noble son.

Ross   Your son, my lord, has paid a soldier's debt:
He only lived but till he was a man,
The which no sooner had his prowess confirmed   **70**
In the unshrinking station where he fought,
But like a man he died.

Siward   Then he is dead?

Ross   Ay, and brought off the field: your cause of sorrow
Must not be measured by his worth, for then
It hath no end.

Siward   Had he his hurts before?   **75**

Ross   Ay, on the front.

Siward   Why then, God's soldier be he!
Had I as many sons as I have hairs,
I would not wish them to a fairer death:
And so his knell is knolled.

Malcolm   He's worth more sorrow,
And that I'll spend for him.

Siward   He's worth no more.   **80**
They say he parted well and paid his score:
And so God be with him! Here comes newer comfort.

[*Re-enter* **Macduff**, *with* **Macbeth**'s *head*]

Macduff   Hail, king! for so thou art. Behold where stands
Th'usurper's head: the time is free:
I see thee compassed with thy kingdom's pearl,   **85**
That speak my salutation in their minds;
Whose voice I desire aloud with mine:
Hail, king of Scotland!

RSC 1988

All   Hail, king of Scotland!

Malcolm   We shall not spend a large expense of time
Before we reckon with your several loves,   90
And make us even with you. My thanes and kinsmen,
Henceforth be earls, the first that ever Scotland
In such an honour named. What's more to do,
Which would be planted newly with the time,
As calling home our exiled friends abroad   95
That fled the snares of watchful tyranny,
Producing forth the cruel ministers
Of this dead butcher and his fiend-like queen,
Who, as 'tis thought, by self and violent hands
Took off her life; this, and what needful else   100
That calls upon us, by the grace of Grace
We will perform in measure, time, and place:
So thanks to all at once, and to each one,
Whom we invite to see us crowned at Scone.

                                        [*Exeunt*]

90-1 reckon . . . you reward you for your individual
        services, and thereby are no longer in your debt
94 which should be established in accordance with the
        changed circumstances
        What do you think is the effect of the horticultural
        metaphor?
97 rooting out and bringing to justice the cruel agents
99 self and violent hands her own violent hands
        Shakespeare is using 'self' as an adjective.
100-1 what . . . us whatever other necessary things
        demand my attention
101 grace of Grace grace of God
102 measure the proper way
103-4 one . . . Scone Elizabethan pronunciation would
        have rhymed these two words.

Is line 98 an adequate obituary for Macbeth
and his wife? Discuss. Write an obituary
notice for either of them: it could be
sympathetic, unsympathetic or balanced,
but you must employ as much as you can of
what you know from the play.

Malcolm's formal – almost ritual – speech
closes the play. How does he present
himself here? Do you think he will make a
good king? Would you want to serve under
him?

Polanski 1971

Sixty Activities and Questions

Below is a list of general activities which can be related to most areas of the play. Activities are also suggested in the marginal notes at specific points in the play where they are most appropriate to the action.

The activities have been deliberately made flexible so that they may be adapted to suit the requirements of the students. The list is not exhaustive, nor is it in any particular order, and ideas do overlap. The activities (or parts of activities) can be used as a basis for discussion, improvisation, written work, revision or whatever is considered important. Most are suitable for individual, paired or group work. The more traditional types of questions are included towards the end of the list, and may also be found among the marginal notes to the play.

1 Produce a speech, an episode, a scene, an act or the whole play.

2 Plan the lighting plot, the set design, the music or the sound for a speech, an episode, a scene, an act or the whole play.

3 Draw up a props list for a scene, an act, or the whole play.

4 As director, write production notes for an actor who has to deliver one of the major speeches of the play. How will you advise him/her to say well-known words as if they are being thought of and spoken for the very first time?

5 As director, write production notes for actors in one episode or scene. Suggest how the actors may try to understand the thoughts and emotions in their own lives. In Act I for instance, Macbeth tells us that his 'function is smothered in surmise' – in other words, he has so much on his mind that he cannot shake himself out of it and get on with what he is supposed to be doing. It is to be hoped that none of us are paralysed into inaction by the evil thoughts in Macbeth's mind, but we may all recognise his general condition. Ask your actors about occasions when their function has been 'smothered in surmise'. Get them to talk about it; or, if they tell you it is too personal to talk about, ask them to think about it and then, perhaps, write down their thoughts as personal writing (not to be shown to anybody).

6 Cast *Macbeth* from one of the following:
a) Well-known actors and actresses. No restriction on choice: you are such a good director that they will all wish to be in your production if you cast them.
b) Well-known public figures. It does not matter if they are not actors: you are casting them because you consider that their physical qualities, voice, manner (and, possibly, your perception of their characters – be careful!) fit the character in the play.
c) Your class.
d) Your friends and relations.

Write a note justifying each piece of casting. For obvious reasons, you may wish to keep lists (c) and (d) private!

7 Write down which part in *Macbeth* you would most like to play, and say why.

8 In order to reduce its length, cut what you consider to be the less important lines from a scene or an act. Write notes justifying those cuts. What has been gained? What has been lost?

9 Rewrite the entire play in modern English in a version to last no longer than 15 minutes. Act it out in improvisation (that is, no scripts).

10 Discuss the significance of any one scene in the structure of the play as a whole.

11 If you have available the 1971 Roman Polanski film version of *Macbeth*, play any one scene and compare it with Shakespeare's text. You will find that Polanski has cut a great deal, often because he has used visual images to take the place of some of the imagery in the original lines. Is he right to do this? What has been gained. What has been lost?

12 Discuss whether Shakespeare is best experienced on stage, on television/video or in the cinema. Is there any point in reading *Macbeth* if you can see it performed?

13 One historical approach: Shakespeare wrote *Macbeth* in honour of the new king of England, James I, who was Scottish. Find out about:
a) the recent events which would have been in people's minds at the time of the first performances of *Macbeth*;

b) the family background and personal interests of King James. Write about the ways in which Shakespeare clearly intended the play to be a tribute to James. You could write in the form of a letter from Shakespeare to the monarch asking permission to come and perform the play before him at his court.

14 Another historical approach: Use the information from 13 above to say in what ways *Macbeth* was a topical play.

15 A further historical approach: Having read about the story of Macbeth in the *Chronicles*, written by a man called Holinshed, Shakespeare altered much of the true history to make his play. For instance, Duncan was young and not a very effective king; Banquo helped Macbeth to kill Duncan; Macbeth then ruled quite well for ten years. Why do you think Shakespeare changed these facts for his play?

Try to find the parts of Holinshed's *Chronicles* which deal with Macbeth (your history teacher should be able to tell you where to find a copy). Compare and contrast his version with Shakespeare's. Does it matter that Shakespeare altered history? Is it important that he did so?

16 Following on from 15, we can see that Shakespeare used other writers as a source for his plays. Discuss in what ways he can still be seen as a great original writer.

17 Invent a card game or board game based on *Macbeth*. It could be based on the rules of an existing game, or you could make it completely original. All hazard cards must bear an appropriate quotation from the play.

(More details of this approach can be found in a journal called *Simulation/Games for Learning*, Volume 15, No 3, edited by Alan Coote, Polytechnic of Wales, Pontypridd, Mid-Glamorgan CF37 1DL.)

18 Write down in no more than one sentence an answer to the question 'What is *Macbeth* about?'. Compare your answers as a way of exploring the dominant themes in the play.

Remember that there is no correct answer, and that your answer, if different to other people's, may lead to just as valid an interpretation of the play. Always ask yourself what lines in the text support your view.

19 Take your idea of the main theme of the play, and write some notes on how it might affect your choice of set design, music, lighting, casting, pacing and other aspects of your production were you to direct the play.

20 Choose one of the photographs or drawings in this book which you found helpful in understanding the play, and give your reasons for choosing it.

21 Choose a photograph which does not fit into your image of the play, and say why you consider it inappropriate.

22 Draw an illustration of any moment in the play which is not illustrated in the book and which you feel is a good subject for illustration.

23 Photographs from various productions are featured in this book. Say which production best fits your image of the play, and give your reasons. If possible, consider all the photographs from your chosen production.

24 See a stage production or a film version of *Macbeth*, and then say how far its interpretation agrees with your view of the play. You could concentrate on one character, theme, scene, episode, speech or idea. Or you could write a straightforward newspaper review of the production.

25 Build a set model for a production of *Macbeth*. It will be for a 'fixed' set: that is, the set remains constant for the whole play, and hence must be flexible and functional for the demands of every scene in the play.

26 Draw up a complete set of costume designs for the play. Be prepared to justify these in terms of your idea of what the play is about and your interpretation of the characters. You may choose to do a modern dress production.

27 Write or improvise a scene of the play which Shakespeare intended to insert into the action, but which he never got round to doing. You could try to write it in a pastiche of Shakespearean language, but if that is too difficult, stick to modern prose. The important thing is to make the events, characters, imagery and so forth consistent with the original play.

28 Design a poster, programme cover, or a whole programme for a production of *Macbeth*.

29 Write a letter from one character to another which might have been written at any point in the play.

30 Imagine that any one of the characters was in the habit of keeping a diary. Write up his/her entry after any one of the scenes in the play.

31 Write a newspaper report which might have been filed at any point in the play. It is important to decide where the journalist was at the time and how he came by his information. Do not include material about which he could not possibly know. When you have finished, give your piece a brief, eye-catching headline.

32 Write a poem in response to any character, theme, episode, moment, or any other aspect of the play. The title of the poem must be a quotation from the play.

33 Make a chart showing in which of the 29 scenes each character appears. Then look closely at the chart and see if you can deduce any ideas about the way Shakespeare has constructed the plot of the play.

34 Characters often spend some time on the stage without speaking. However, as human beings they will continue to think, particularly if the events enacted before them are in any way remarkable.
a) Write an 'inner monologue' for any one of the characters in which we see what he/she is thinking during one of the episodes in the play.
b) Write notes for the actor who is to play your chosen character, advising him how to register his thoughts during the episode (remember that acting is more than merely talking).

35 'Translate' part of a scene into modern English. Try to retain both the meaning and the 'feel' of the original.

36 Write an obituary notice for any of the characters. You could write about one who dies during the course of *Macbeth*, in which case you must stick to the known facts of the play; or you could write on a character who survives the play, in which case you may imagine what happens to him in later life, but you must remain consistent to his character as established in *Macbeth*.

37 Think of as many *very brief* quotations as you can which are said by, or about one of the characters. Then say how each quotation is significant.

38 Choose a character which you would like to play and prepare one of his/her speeches for audition. Use a tape-recorder and mirror to practise, and pay particular attention to tone of voice, pacing of the speech, and facial gesture.

39 Make a quotation list comprising what you consider to be the ten most powerful images in *Macbeth*. Then, in the light of this list, discuss your impression of the overall tone of the play.

40 If there is a castle near you, visit it and, while you are going round, imagine the events of *Macbeth* taking place there. A group of you could take copies of the text and rehearse a scene in that setting.

41 Invite an actor or director who has been concerned with a production of *Macbeth* to come and talk about the experience.

42 Write a review of the first night of *Macbeth* in the Globe theatre. You could include comments on how the Jacobean audience received the play.

43 Write out the transcript of an interview with William Shakespeare, who is pleased with the favourable reception at the first night of his new play. You could brief one of your friends to play the part of Shakespeare in the interview and, like many journalists, use a tape-recorder to record the conversation.

44 Take any line in the play and practise saying it in different ways, varying the words upon which you place stress. Consider which version you think most satisfactory, and say why.

45 What Shakespeare wrote in his plays were the thoughts and opinions of his characters, not of himself. However, we can see from a play such as *Macbeth* the breadth of his knowledge and understanding.

Take a speech, episode, scene, act or the whole play and with close reference to the text show what we can deduce about Shakespeare's knowledge and understanding.

46 Say in what ways Shakespeare has encouraged his audience to use its imagination. Look closely at the language of *Macbeth*.

47 Examine closely any one soliloquy in the play, and then discuss the dramatic functions of soliloquies. How are they useful in putting over what dialogue cannot do?

48 Discuss what you mean by 'tragedy'. In what sense is *Macbeth* a tragedy? Is Macbeth himself a tragic figure? Or should he be dismissed as a 'dead butcher'? Is Lady Macbeth tragic? Human? Or can she be summed up as 'fiend-like'?

49 Discuss whether there is any comedy in *Macbeth*. If so, where – and why is it there?

50 Which two characters in the play do you find most interesting? Why? Do you find them and their actions understandable? Do you feel that you want to judge them, or can you view them with compassion? Do you sympathise with them? Can you go as far as identifying (empathising) with them – that is, can you, so to speak, climb inside them and know what it is to go around with their thoughts, hopes, anxieties, fears, etc., in your head?

51 Choose any illustration in this edition which has no caption. Then search the text of the play to find a suitable caption.

52 Learn a speech from a part for which you would like to audition. Write it down from memory. Recite it from memory. Then act it out as if for an audition for your chosen part.

53 Write out a speech from the play and then scan it, putting accent marks over the syllables which you think should be stressed.

54 Choose any 14 lines from the play and rewrite them in good modern English.

55 *Macbeth* can be very exciting in performance. Which two incidents in the play would you select as particularly dramatic? Support your choice with detailed reference.

56 For all its power, *Macbeth* often fails in performance. Write director's notes to your cast pointing out to them the danger-points where the play could fail.

57 Show how Shakespeare's poetry helps to create the right atmosphere for the violent events of the play.

58 'Ambition and treachery are the main themes of the play.' Discuss.

59 Recite (not necessarily from memory) your favourite lines from *Macbeth*. Say why you like them.

60 In what ways may the play be said to be a struggle between the forces of good and evil?

Notes on Productions of *Macbeth* Illustrated in this Edition

Crucible Theatre 1985
Director: Mike Kay • Macbeth: Brian Protheroe • Lady Macbeth: Margot Leicester • Banquo: Martin Duncan • Malcolm: Will Tacey • Macduff: Stuart Richman

For further information contact: Publicity Officer, Crucible Theatre, 55 Norfolk Street, Sheffield S1 1DA, Tel: 0742 760621

Great Eastern Stage 1985
Director: Ian McKeand • Macbeth: Barry McGuin • Lady Macbeth: Terry Diab • Banquo: Fraser Wilson • Macduff: Maurice Perry

For further information contact: Publicity Officer, Great Eastern Stage, Steinkirk Building, Dunkirk Road, Lincoln LN1 3UJ, Tel: 0522 34924

Leicester Haymarket 1985
Director: Nancy Meckler • Macbeth: Bernard Hill • Lady Macbeth: Julie Walters • Banquo: Joseph Marcell • Malcolm: Jeremy Swift • Macduff: Nick Stringer

For further information contact: Publicity Officer, Leicester Haymarket Theatre, Belgrave Gate, Leicester LE1 3QY, Tel: 0533 530021

National Theatre 1978
Director: Peter Hall (with John Russell Brown) • Macbeth: Albert Finney • Lady Macbeth: Dorothy Tutin • Banquo: Robin Bailey • Malcolm: Nicky Henson • Macduff: Daniel Massey

For further information contact: Publicity Officer, National Theatre, South Bank, London SE1 9PX, Tel: 01-928 2033

New Victoria Theatre 1966
Director: Peter Cheeseman • Macbeth: Ron Daniels • Lady Macbeth: Angela Galbraith • Banquo: Terence Davies • Malcolm: Christopher Martin • Macduff: Anton Vogel

New Victoria Theatre 1976
Director: Clare R Venables • Macbeth: Bruce Alexander • Lady Macbeth: Polly Warren • Banquo: Nick Darke • Malcolm: James Masters • Macduff: Bernard Latham

For further information contact: Publicity Officer, New Victoria Theatre, Etruria Road, Newcastle-under-Lyme ST5 0JG, Tel: 0782 717539

Northcott Theatre 1986
Director: George Roman • Macbeth: Pip Miller • Lady Macbeth: Nina Holloway • Banquo: Michael Gunn • Malcolm: Benedict Blythe • Macduff: Eugene Lipinski

For further information contact: Publicity Officer, Northcott Theatre, Stocker Road, Exeter EX4 4QB, Tel: 0392 56182

Oxford Playhouse 1982 (now known as Oxford Stage Company)
Director: Gordon McDougall • Macbeth: Tim Hardy • Lady Macbeth: Ann Firbank • Banquo: Mark Penfold • Malcolm: Richard Cottan • Macduff: David Lyon

For further information contact: Publicity Officer, Oxford Stage Company, 12 Beaumont Street, Oxford OX 1 2LW, Tel: 0865 723238

Polanski 1971 (Columbia Pictures Industries Inc.)
Director: Roman Polanski • Macbeth: Jon Finch • Lady Macbeth: Francesca Annis • Banquo: Martin Shaw • Malcolm: Stephan Chase

For further information contact: Publicity Officer, Columbia Pictures Corporation Ltd, 19 Wells Street, London W1, Tel: 01-580 2090

Royal Lyceum 1986
Director: Jules Wright • Macbeth: Jonathon Hyde • Lady Macbeth: Julie Covington • Banquo: John Bett • Malcolm: Christopher Bowen • Macduff: Barrie Rutter

For further information contact: Publicity Officer, Royal Lyceum Theatre, Grindlay Street, Edinburgh EH3 9AX, Tel: 031-229 7404

RSC 1974
Director: Trevor Nunn • Macbeth: Nicol Williamson • Lady Macbeth: Helen Mirren • Banquo: Barry Stanton • Malcolm: Eric Allen • Macduff: Malcolm Tierney

RSC 1976 (at The Other Place, Stratford-upon-Avon)
Director: Trevor Nunn • Macbeth: Ian McKellen • Lady Macbeth: Judi Dench • Banquo: John Woodvine • Malcolm: Roger Rees • Macduff: Bob Peck

RSC 1982
Director: Howard Davies • Macbeth: Bob Peck • Lady Macbeth: Sara Kestelman • Banquo: Malcolm Storry • Malcolm: Chris Hunter • Macduff: Pete Postlethwaite

RSC 1986
Director: Adrian Noble • Macbeth: Jonathan Pryce • Lady Macbeth: Sinead Cusak • Banquo: Hugh Quarshie • Malcolm: Nicholas Woodeson • Macduff: Peter Guinness

RSC 1988
Director: Adrian Noble • Macbeth: Miles Anderson • Lady Macbeth: Amanda Root • Banquo: Tony Armatrading • Malcolm: Duncan Bell • Macduff: Colin McCormack

For further information contact: Publicity Officer, Royal Shakespeare Theatre, Stratford-upon-Avon, Warwickshire CV37 6BB, Tel: 0789 296655, *or* The Shakespeare Birthplace Trust, The Shakespeare Centre, Henley Street, Stratford-upon-Avon CV37 6QW, Tel: 0789 204016

Torch Theatre 1986
Director: Les Miller • Macbeth: Rob Dixon • Lady Macbeth: Joanne Foster • Banquo: Gary Lilburn • Malcolm: Mark Draper • Macduff: Peter Glaney

For further information contact: Publicity Officer, Torch Theatre, St Peter's Road, Milford Haven, Dyfed SA73 2BW, Tel: 06462 4192

Young Vic 1984
Director: David Thacker • Macbeth: Malcolm Tierney • Lady Macbeth: Margot Leicester • Banquo: T-Bone Wilson • Malcolm: Brian Bovell • Macduff: Jeffrey Kissoon

For further information contact: Publicity Officer, The Young Vic, 66 The Cut, London SE1 8LZ, Tel: 01-633 0133